INTERVIEW
with
YOUR SELF

Be Inner-Wise,
Resolve Life's Problems

MERCEDES TUR ESCRIVA

BALBOA.
PRESS
A DIVISION OF HAY HOUSE

Balboa Press books may be ordered through booksellers or by contacting:

Balboa Press
A Division of Hay House
1663 Liberty Drive
Bloomington, IN 47403
www.balboapress.com
1 (877) 407-4847

Because of the dynamic nature of the Internet, any web addresses or links contained in this book may have changed since publication and may no longer be valid. The views expressed in this work are solely those of the author and do not necessarily reflect the views of the publisher, and the publisher hereby disclaims any responsibility for them.

The author of this book does not dispense medical advice or prescribe the use of any technique as a form of treatment for physical, emotional, or medical problems without the advice of a physician, either directly or indirectly. The intent of the author is only to offer information of a general nature to help you in your quest for emotional and spiritual well-being. In the event you use any of the information in this book for yourself, which is your constitutional right, the author and the publisher assume no responsibility for your actions.

Any people depicted in stock imagery provided by Thinkstock are models, and such images are being used for illustrative purposes only. Certain stock imagery © Thinkstock.

Printed in the United States of America.

ISBN: 978-1-4525-1985-2 (sc)
ISBN: 978-1-4525-1987-6 (hc)
ISBN: 978-1-4525-1986-9 (e)

Library of Congress Control Number: 2014914277

Balboa Press rev. date: 11/12/2014

1st Edition by Jami Lynn Sands

Contents

APPENDICES

Preface

The urge to write this book came from contemplating how society is changing, and how, in the process, many people are suffering painfully It was born of a sense of frustration and the need to share my story with others.

Initially, I began writing this book in Spanish. Looking back now, it was the beginning of a series of events that were completely out of my control. At that time, I was working for a US corporation and single and free of family obligations. I had the time and felt the need to do something for others. It was as if I was being led to write and share the ideas and concepts I had learned through my studies, travels, and experiences. It had been a painful journey back to my inner self. My dream of being able to earn a living with what my heart desired most, being a practicing psychologist, seemed to be broken into pieces. At that point, I was lost and unsure of my role in the world. I had to close my practice, a lovely well-being center complete with a flotarium, as well as yoga and Ayurveda facilities.

I had invested my heart, my energy, and all of my savings in a project that would have me remortgage my home and enslave me even more to an unfulfilling job in corporate America. In my desperation, I kept asking myself why life seemed so unfair. I never had a partner or children, which had been my heart's desire as a young woman. That dream had gone unfulfilled, and now I had to close down my space and heal my wounds once again. For several years, I felt like a failure.

My goal is to share what I have learned in order to help others understand the process of change, as well as how to gain a new perspective. What I have learned from these experiences has helped me to move away from pain and suffering. Throughout the process, I moved out of my comfort zone, those areas in my life that somehow made me feel secure, but at a high price. During those times, I was living a life that made no sense to me. Although the value of the experiences was priceless, there was still much that needed to come through. The feeling of wanting to share and help others was increasing gradually every day. However, I was not sure about how *powerless little me* could do anything that would be of real value to others.

The strikes in the cities, the congregations of masses of people in the streets of the big cities, the banks taking back people's homes, and families that have only milk for dinner are all too painful to watch. The one thing that really broke my heart was seeing all the pain that those readjusting at a social, economic, and spiritual level were enduring. It felt like someone was squeezing my heart; I felt constant pressure in my chest. What could I do alone? Broke financially, feeling helpless like everyone else, I was living a life that amounted to nothing but a mortgage and living with only my small pet. Little did I know that I, too, was going to be swept away once again from my dreams and be brought back into a survival mode just like everyone else around me.

The universe, however, had conspired to arrange the time for me to contemplate, organize my thoughts, and then provided the perfect circumstances for me to write it down. Things started to get hard for me at work. They were implementing changes, and somehow my job description did not fit their plans any longer. After four months of being pushed around and tested to my limits, I was laid off. At the time, I could not fully understand; things do not always make sense to us when they are happening. In retrospect, I now know I was at the right place at the right time.

My initial response was fear and panic and I became depressed. A few months into this new set of circumstances, I recalled how earlier, I had a strong desire to have a sabbatical year. This time would allow me to do what I wanted: write, study, and do my own thing. However, I had never been out of a job before, so my first response was to start looking at ways to continue my business, take courses online, and get back into my Ayurvedic psychology practice. Things were moving very slowly at work and it was turning into a draining task that, needless to say, did not pay my bills. This was largely because I offered my services for free, since I did have a check coming in from social support services. I was still better off than many of my clients. However, when the memory of my wished-for sabbatical year crossed my mind, I thought, I have created this situation; how can I use this time and opportunity for the good of all? I began to relax, go for walks, and little by little, got myself back together.

With the dawning of the New Year 2013, alone with my dog and still jobless, I decided that my mission for the New Year was to stop the struggle and to teach others how to do the same. Over the months, I had been given signs from everywhere that this book was supposed to be. Emails from people and companies I did not know landed in my mailbox. I enrolled in a mentorship program. I felt that I wanted to be part of something else that I could not find around me.

During my first mentorship call, I was encouraged and it was as if something higher than myself also approved. My mission seemed to be supported by a continuous stream of events that have not stopped. Our lives are a succession of events that lead us to the fulfillment of our strongest desires. I initially understood mine as a desire to understand the human mind and its behaviors. That was the force that initially drove me to pursue my psychology degree. It was complicated, first, because English is my second language. Secondly, as a night student, I still had to support myself with a full-time day job for a Spanish company based in the UK.

After my graduation, I enrolled in the British Psychological Society where I served as a board member of the North of England Branch for a couple of years. I was unsure as to what the next step in my higher education would be. At the time, I honestly believed that academics and the sciences had all the answers. I was already becoming disenchanted with the mainstream approach to human behavior and the mind. The *DSM* (*Diagnostic Manual of Psychology*) did not make any sense when compared with my experience of schizophrenia in my own family. I thought perhaps my Masters in Music Therapy would change that; the truth was, it did not. Because I had not received a satisfactory response to many more complicated questions, I began a personal quest to find answers to the questions myself.

The understanding of the cognitive processes and the biology and chemistry of the brain did provide much useful information, but only part of it. It seemed to be too scientific and mechanical. It also left me seriously confused as to why we are always in search of proof for everything. It made no sense why some concepts were accepted and others would not even be mentioned. For example, isn't the existence of the ego inferred? Yes it is, but why can we not infer with regard to other subjects?

An important concept to examine was the existence of God, along with the meaning of certain passages of the Holy Scriptures. I certainly felt the pressure to be objective, as a psychologist would need to be. For example, I could freely comment on theology and how it has impacted the history and behavior of humans for thousands of years, but not much else. As a result of not wanting to pick on these precepts, I was drawn into the philosophies of the East, practices like meditation and its effect on the human experience and mind. I was not really into the esoteric, religious, or dogmatic disciplines, but there is plenty to choose from in the East. Hence, I started a road of self-discovery without realizing it. This book has come about after years of reading, studying Ayurvedic medicine, and the *I Ching*, as well as trying different techniques for personal and spiritual development. It summarizes what has worked for my many clients and for me.

Introduction

How many books on self-development, spirituality, and wisdom must one read to live in balance? Why do we forget them so fast and go back to our old ways? Must we keep going to workshops and forever feel that more and more work is required? There are multiple answers to those questions—all valid. Yet I reached a point where I needed to find my own voice, my own way of applying my understanding of life and the things that matter most. If you are like me, you have been reading inspirational books on self-development and looking for answers to a long list of personal, spiritual, and social questions and needs. If this is so, know that you are in good company. This book is an introduction to a process of self-inquiry that will help to guide you towards your true self. If you have a strong desire to live a life in balance with your soul's purpose, this is a good start. If you have already begun this journey, this can be a productive next step in the process. This book could change the way you experience life every day.

As we enter a new paradigm, we are changing our definition and vision of the human experience. Therefore, we must also enter it with new tools. These will allow the transition to be easy and intimate, providing a strong sense of clarity and well-being about the changes in progress. The interview process described herein is for everyone, even if you already consider yourself to be on a spiritual path. This process can be integrated at any time, whether you are someone who has used meditation, other techniques, or are new to spiritual practices. Perhaps you just want to get more clarity in your thinking process. This book offers different points of view and additional ideas to further explore. The promise of this book is to offer you tools to use, and if you employ them, they will create a deep, inner connection with your wise inner self. You'll better understand your mental process and its relationship with each part of your being.

Since I introduced spiritual practices into my life, everything has become more authentic, more fun, and more real. The most exciting part, however, has been that I feel a connection to a higher body of knowledge that I can relate to and trust deeply. I will also share with you what I have come to understand through my experiences with the *I Ching*, Ayurveda, yoga, and other disciplines and traditions. I will include insights that have been revealed to me through my soul, as well as others that have come to me in the form of teachings.

We do not realize how simple life can be. This is partly due to our programmed beliefs and ideas—concepts that we hardly ever question. We make many assumptions, thereby making choices based solely on the beliefs and judgments of others, past and future. We often do not realize how many of these premises may not be valid or real when applied to the situation we are facing. For example, I was discussing in a coaching session how a difficult encounter with a person we love can distort our true feelings for them. We argue and then we feel hurt, which (most of the time) leads us to respond in a given way. While wearing our feelings on our sleeves, we often fail to see how these negative emotions will most likely result in recreating more of the same. Sometimes we have to force ourselves to detach from a situation physically and emotionally. Each time we do this, it provides a space for other, more positive energies and thoughts to enter. In my case, it made me walk away from a confrontation that was never going to benefit anyone involved. It provided the needed space for the two of us to think. I came to realize that it is always better to be happy than to be right.

We place a high value on happiness, but we so readily let go of it, only to satisfy our egos, which includes self-image and self-specialness. Happiness and modesty are precious; they can help us to feel grounded and balanced. It is sometimes difficult to maintain this state of mind and stay in balance, particularly when we do not believe it is possible or because a new idea or a new emotion enters our space. Most of the time this is an unconscious process usually formed by unquestioned thoughts, beliefs, or desires, all of which turn into a self-fulfilling prophecy.

As a young adult, all I wished for was happiness—nothing else. As the years went by, I came to believe that happiness was very hard to come by, that, in fact, it never lasted and that it meant having to do a lot of work to achieve it. My perception of happiness was based on external things providing this state of being rather than my inner self making it manifest. It is the realization of the latter, not the former, that provides true happiness for extended periods of time. Sometimes it only comes after a long road full of difficult turns and failures. These life experiences supply us with a first-hand understanding, knowledge, and a new vision of the world and of ourselves. They allow us to reassess what we truly want to create next in our lives.

This book is a guide to be used to bring clarity to your thinking process, designed to be especially helpful when you are moving through difficult times. It will provide you with a way to reach your wise inner self, your soul. With the interview process, you will regain balance every time you move away from your authentic, wise, inner voice. Use it to help you find your own unique responses to the events and situations that create resistance and imbalance in your life. The questions are designed to assist you in gaining a clear vision and understanding of what is meant by body, mind, and soul and to see their interactions in your everyday life. Please check the glossary for terms with which you may be unfamiliar.

Interview with Your Self is about finding our inner truth and being true, not only to others, but to one's self. A peaceful, balanced life requires a good dose of authenticity and loyalty to our wise inner self.

In my work with people I acknowledge that each individual has the correct answer inside. My role is merely one of helping them to access it. The book provides a powerful interviewing tool. The interview allows the enquiry to go into three different levels of looking at the same situation: the level of the body (material), the mind (logical process), and the level of the soul (wise self). The process allows for clarity to emerge that only the person in the situation can access, a clarity that is in balance with the broader scheme of things. It promotes trust and understanding of how to manage the situation at hand.

Clarity has a healing power that encourages the larger truth to emerge with new visions that are less constricted by the limited ego vision of the world. It is part of a process that enriches life and relationships. We come to understand that each of us has to undergo the very same process and that no one is better (or worse) equipped on this journey. We have everything we need inside of us; there is no need to look outside of ourselves.

Our knowledge has been taught to us; our wisdom is within us.

Chapter 1

DOES YOUR LIFE MAKE SENSE?

What is happening in the world? I do not pretend to be able to respond or provide satisfying answers to that question. I can only share my own answers with you. In fact, this will apply to all findings presented here; because they are my own unique perspective, they may not necessarily be yours. We are living in fast-changing times, what some would call "declining times." When we look around us, it seems we are in the middle of the collapse of established systems and structures that we believed were solid and secure not so long ago.

It is hard to believe that what is happening all over the world is a positive change. We are witnessing the closing of yet another chapter in human history. From our observation of major, significant shifts in the economic, political, social, environmental, and religious structures in most countries on the planet, we can conclude that the current state of our lives has been cocreated by humans through our collective consciousness. There is plenty of information online that addresses any questions we might have, but can any of it provide the answers we all seek?

The truth of the matter is that we can all make some sense of these events by reaching inside ourselves for our individual answers. In turn, this would help us to provide a better course of action and response to these events, based on how they touch each of us. The fact that you are reading this book tells me that you are interested in creating a new or better life for yourself and your loved ones. The reasons vary from individual to individual, but the process is basically the same for each of us: change is inevitable. Whether we like it or not, we are all changing with the times. It would be very helpful to understand what change is and why it takes place.

The main focus of this book are to help you find your uniqueness, and to provide information that can assist you in reaching inside of yourself for your own personal, authentic answers. I have become increasingly aware that people already have the responses they are looking for within themselves. Most of the time, they only need a little guidance to find them. We get so entangled with our thoughts, egos, and the dynamics of the mind that we fail to see that we have everything we need within our reach. When we detach completely from these mental blocks standing in the way, we find a new dimension to our lives that is rich in knowledge and support.

Our society promises fast fixes for almost everything. Therefore, when we look at our problems, we tend to look for a fast fix. This usually comes from our past experiences, or some conceptual knowledge, information, or reasoning. Sometimes we get things fixed, sometimes not. From my own experience and from talking to many clients, it appears that when we rush into fixing a situation, we miss the possibility of connecting to our source. This connection could have provided a more authentic response. In identifying that connection, we could learn to avoid facing the same situation repeatedly.

The urgency to solve problems stems from fear and a deep feeling of mistrust. We believe that we need to do something about the situation here and now; otherwise, this or that will happen. The feeling of urgency is due mostly to our evolutionary fight-or-flight response. We developed these instincts and acted or reacted during the days when our ancestors were often in danger. There was no time to reflect; to survive, the correct response was required as soon as a potential threat or danger was perceived. Even though the vast majority of our current daily situations no longer require us to choose to run, fight, or die, our reaction is still driven by this primal response mechanism whenever we feel fear or are threatened. However, the truth is that now, we do have time to respond, we do have time to reflect, and we do have time to be genuine with ourselves.

Having the space to think things over, meditate, and connect to our source is of vital importance. This always provides us with more authentic responses, ones that do not come from a place of duality, and black or white. Instead, these are responses that find either a middle ground or an alternate route. These are responses that you could not have conceived of if you had not given yourself the time and space. The responses come from a place beyond our likes and dislikes and our personal shortsighted desires and needs. This is what I call "the source" inside of each of us. That is why when we come from that source in ourselves, we are authentic to ourselves and to others. What we do is more appropriate and universally benign. These types of responses are required now in our world, if we are to create the world that we all want in the coming years. We need to reach the space inside of us that is in communion with our larger self.

When put into practice, the insight and techniques offered here will assist you in getting to your own truth. If we all searched inside of ourselves, we would come to the same place—a place of love. Nothing else besides love is possible; everything that shows up to oppose love has been born out of confusion and a misunderstanding of what is real, the source, love.

For thousands of years, the sages have maintained that the world is an illusion projected by the ego, our intellectual mind. Over the passage of time, scientists have proven that the observer *creates* reality. The issue that now arises is why are we creating this reality? First of all, it has been cocreated from the start, and secondly, we must agree that the only time we should proceed or act on something is when it benefits the whole of humanity, hence, also benefiting us. However, that is not what we are generally taught. If we notice that something is not benefiting the whole, neither will it ultimately prove to be beneficial to oneself. One does not require a degree from a university to know this; it just requires more information and time before we decide "what is what." We must get clear on what is an illusion, and what is real. This scenario brings to mind the title of David Bowie's song, "The Man Who Sold the World." The title needs no further explanation; it says it all.

Having money is not synonymous with having success or happiness. A millionaire may still worry about money and how to continue to keep his expensive lifestyle going. If he can afford to do that, then his mind will turn toward other desirable objects, such as more power, health, love, or youth. The basic needs are the same all across the human race, and are not related to physical things. We have physical needs, but it is just as important to recognize that we also have spiritual needs. Our physical needs should be in alignment with our spiritual needs in order to experience the joys of life.

The world tells us we need the physical, material things in life in order to be happy. However, we are now facing a world that is really at the brink of creating a new paradigm, where our spiritual lives and our physical lives become one and are nonexclusive.

Many have come to realize the transitory nature of material things, our roles, and even power. We come to understand that there is something else we want to achieve, something that is more authentic and enduring. This is why authenticity is so important. You would not want to wake up in fifteen years to discover that everything you have been chasing after is false or a fairy tale. Maybe you have already reached that point; if so, please do not despair. I assure you life will change that too. Some things will never leave us, because they are inside of us and away from time and space. These are the true treasures of life, the ones we cannot afford to do without.

Adversity

What about, if we never again forget that every moment of decay is also one of creation?.

Adversity provides us with the opportunity to understand what it is we really value. It is part of the organic process of creation and destruction in the universe. It is also by this process that we ourselves create and deconstruct and get to experience firsthand what it is that we truly are and truly want. The *truth* is always there; we just need to be prepared to see it. That is the opportunity adversity provides us. It creates the perfect situation to help us, in any given moment, see what our truth is.

These concepts have been expressed by many wise spiritual teachers and counselors over time. This is precisely my interpretation of the hidden message lying behind all the events taking place on a social scale at any given moment in history. Some propose that we need to get to a critical mass so that we make a quantum leap to a more evolved model of human consciousness. Personally, I believe that we are not far from this point now. I am happy to see signs of this in many of the social networks.

From looking at human history, one can conclude that consciousness has always been evolving, and it develops from the inside, from our source. I am not referring to the consciousness traditionally expressed by various views of human evolution. I specifically refer to our treasured and rediscovered ideas on spirituality. In order to build a better world, we must experience and integrate these into our lives as a living *organic process.* The evolution of consciousness is not something outside of ourselves that only a few humans can reach. True understanding does not come from a conceptual point of view or from mere information. True understanding comes from experience; there is a difference between *knowing* something and *being* something. Spiritual evolution involves *being* in the moment. We are all involved in the evolution of consciousness, whether we are aware of it or not. We do this all the time by the process of changing our thinking patterns, which creates new neuronal pathways. These come about through an organic process taking place in our brain. These pathways are created by repeating our thought patterns continuously; we do it constantly without even realizing it. In order to become conscious, one must start to create new patterns by connecting daily with one's wise inner self.

We all have the right to enjoy our lives and to be happy and fulfilled as we proceed on this journey called life. We do this by creating changes at an unconscious level; this allows us to experience higher levels of understanding. At times, it requires that we step out of our comfort zone— willingly or not.

In the Chinese language, the symbol that represents the word crisis is the same symbol used to represent the word opportunity. To embrace a perspective that allows you to understand the movement of life and everything that is, means to feel less threatened by sources of fear. It may be the end of a job, the threat of an illness, or the loss of a loved one; it may also be a business, a home, or a relationship. It's often a combination of several of these factors. When you are faced with difficult or challenging times, you must make the decision to act or react. It will define how any given situation is going to affect you. If the decision is free of emotional responses, such as fear, you stand a better chance of being able to use it to your good and that of others. Once you make the decision not to respond automatically without reflection, you open your heart and mind to an input flow that comes from your wise inner self. You will then experience a synchronicity of events that will move you forward in a positive direction. Most importantly, by maintaining a detached attitude, you can be more receptive to your unique, personal view of how you would prefer to live from this moment on.

By employing detachment in a positive way, you base your life on your desire to be true to your inner self and your authentic soul. Furthermore, you will be able to conceive a new life situation for yourself. It will match what is in harmony with you and with the world. It is that process that defines for us our lives' purposes.

Understanding Change

Change is all there is and it will always be the condition of our world. From the perspective of ancient wisdom, life is like a flowing river. We must understand that life is an organic process. The Rishis in India more than 3,000 years ago understood this process; their knowledge and visions are described in their scriptures, the *Vedas*. We can find many of the same principles in the *Tao Te Ching* from the Chinese; other ancient holy books also support this view of life. These teachings understood that the universe was an on-going process of creation and decay. Their vision is now partly shared by physicists who study the laws of creation and decay (Thermodynamics). Paradoxically our scientists (just as the sages) have not yet provided many of the answers to these age-old questions about life.

In our scientific understanding of the world, there is a point where we realize we do not have all the answers; therefore, it becomes necessary to accept the existence of paradox and ambiguity. By allowing ourselves to experience that same element of uncertainty in our own lives, we come to know first-hand that nothing is certain or lasts forever. The constant tension in the universe created by the interaction of creation and disintegration still remains a mystery to us on both a large and small scale.

If we add to this paradox the findings of quantum mechanics (science that studies the micro world of atoms and small pieces of matter) on the quantum field, we get to a point that all of existence is an empty vacuum or empty space. Moreover, this vacuum space is known to consist of energy and information, which then reveals that the space is not empty at all. I will expand more on what this has to do with us and what the energy and information mean in the next sub-chapter, as well as in Chapter 7.

Obviously, one can conclude from this that nothing ever really disintegrates, but merely changes form. This is a view shared by the ancient sages and other belief systems throughout the world. All matter has to undergo the process of decay, so its form is changing constantly. Although impossible for the average human mind to perceive, physicists are also aware that things can be in more than one place at a time. Through the *Tao*, we are given the message that we cannot understand everything there is to know, nor can we change the forces that operate at will; neither should we care. Its teachings encourage us to accept and rest peacefully with the uncertain nature of things.

It can be said that change is an ongoing mechanism or process. There is a major order for things, an order that we still do not fully understand. Moreover, we will come to live in peace only when we fully accept the necessity of uncertainty in our lives. Can you imagine your life with everything secure and certain, with everything under control, down to every single little detail? What if you never had to endure any adversity and uncertainty? Do you think that would be positive for you? Go inside yourself and imagine your life like that—all certain, secure, and risk free.

The philosopher Kierkegaard wrote, "One should not think slightingly of the paradoxical; for the paradox is the source of the thinker's passion, and the thinker without a paradox is like a lover without a feeling: a paltry mediocrity" (*The Frankfurt School of Religion*, p. 157). Could you then conceive your life without ambiguity?

Is All Energy in Motion, Even Our Thoughts?

Scientists recognize that nothing changes until something moves. When we bring these truths to a micro level, we see that there is constant movement; even in a field of nothing, something is always happening. Everything is changing; nothing has an established form or existence forever. Everything is therefore moving from here to there and from there to here. That movement is sometimes expressed as the wheel or circle of life—the cycle of creation and destruction. It only undergoes a transformation process in order to express itself in another form of existence within the wheel. These beliefs have long lived within the minds of many, especially those of Eastern cultures who also believe in reincarnation. Someone once asked the Dalai Lama about the big bang, to which he responded, "Which one?"

In recent times much emphasis has been placed on the power of thought and how we become what we think about. Although this is valuable insight, it has created an internal battle in many people. We cannot stop our thoughts from coming; they are like clouds in the sky (discussed in Chapter 4), but we can change the impact they have on us by simply observing those thoughts and deciding upon which of them to act.

Some thoughts have a more powerful energy and impact than others. So we need to learn what to do with these thoughts before they gain force and create feelings and emotions that are not aligned with our higher selves. No thought has ultimate control over us; we always have power over them, but we must get clear on the thought and its pattern. Thoughts are like clouds; sometimes they carry a lot of rain and the elements combine in a way to produce a perfect storm. However, we are the ones who make the decision as to how we handle it when we are in a storm. Remember, the calm is always waiting ahead.

Our truth is always inside of us, although at times it is blocked by cloudy skies. If we can be true to our knowledge and understanding during change, we will be able to avoid unnecessary suffering and focus on how we respond.

In the *I Ching*, we reflect on two types of internal truth. The first one comes from our thoughts and powerfully creates our external world in a positive or negative manner. The second is related to an important aspect of the truth that is sometimes beyond our control. It is related to seeing the bigger scheme of things, and is understood to be the essence of the truth in a given situation. Moreover, it is this truth that has the power to heal everything, to illuminate every aspect of situations, and to manifest things in the physical world. I know it seems a little too esoteric, but when perceived, it changes everything, opens doors, and out of nowhere, creates what seemed impossible only twenty-four hours ago. It's hard to explain, but if you have ever experienced this, you do not need further explanation. It is these truths about our lives that we have a tendency to discharge and forget; yet these are the truths we should never forget. These are the truths that operate at an internal level. If we can embrace such ideas and concepts, we will experience a complete change in our perception of life and its meaning. Furthermore, we can relax and seek answers to questions without that sense of urgency or neediness that normally accompanies our questioning of everyday life.

Review: Just by remembering life is change and that it is an organic process, we will know that nothing is permanent. As we question the situations in our lives during the process of interviewing ourselves, we will slowly and gradually discover that nothing is so important or so urgent.

That is the hidden treasure of the interview process. It's a kind of reflective questioning that allows you to gain a new vision—a more authentic one of what is in front of you.

Why do we need to question ourselves in the first place? It's because most, if not all, of the information we consider to be valid is based on assumptions, beliefs, and interpretations, as well as emotions. More often than not, you will see that the thoughts are not based on the real facts or truths of who you are. They often come from past experiences or social beliefs we might not be in agreement with anymore. Sometimes we are not even fully aware of their source. For example, we tend to respond to external events after thinking and identifying recognizable patterns; this makes sense according to our experience. This is not a problem if the experience is the same now or if we responded to it correctly in the past. People often do something because they believe it reflects what they are, do, or feel. As a result, they keep facing the same unwanted situations. This is a good example of why we need to question ourselves. Sometimes it is the only way to come up with the correct and authentic response to what is really happening. Many other possible scenarios can affect the response, such as confusing this moment with a previous moment. Although the two appear at first glance to be the same, they are not. Discovering the differences will assist us in finding a new way of responding to the situation.

The fact is that we do this questioning all the time; we are just not aware that we are doing it because it is done in an automatic mode. We do not consider that in some instances (if not most), the obvious response will be heavily influenced by the past, as well as our beliefs and emotions. Using the interview as a tool is powerful. However, it's not a new tool; it has made humans overcome many obstacles. I've found that when I do this with clients or myself, clarity always surfaces to a certain extent and we are able to detach ourselves from the results to some degree.

Although we may have reached a point where we are conscious of how we are manifesting our thoughts and that we, ourselves, are creating our lives and our worlds, we still may not be using the tools within our power to their full potential. This is simply because we have been led to believe that the most important tools are outside of us.

A little less suffering each day on our part contributes to eliminating the pain and suffering of the collective consciousness in the world. Imagine how you will feel and interact with others when you are free of pain, full of love, and have that vision in mind that nothing is more important than how you think and feel. It creates more of the same wherever you show up; there you are—full of love.

Chapter 2

WE ARE ALL ONE

The ego is a term widely used and from a humble point of view, I believe it is misunderstood. Most people do not understand its spiritual purpose. Therefore, in our world the ego has a bad reputation, which creates internal conflict. This can only be resolved if we see that the ego is not us or who we are, but forms the characteristics that differentiate *me* from the rest. Still, many people only identify with their physical bodies and egos (that part of our minds that gives us our senses of self-worth), and not with the force that empowers these two parts of the self. We have heard of the spiritual phrase, *we are all one*, but the meaning is still not widely understood. We are all one, and in that sense, we are all part of a larger body. We are individual parts, each having our own set of likes and dislikes, as well as talents and weakness. What does it mean to have a spirit, a living intelligent energy force, a soul, or whatever you want to call it? Our DNA knows this better than we do. All of our cells have the information they need to express and accomplish their tasks within the human body. We grasp these concepts because we've seen their mode of operation and roles in our bodies. Can we open our minds now and see this on a bigger scale? You will find that if you truly open your mind to such a concept, evidence of it will come to you from many sources—so many that you will not doubt again.

We need to understand who we are and what we are made of instead of engaging in an ongoing battle with our egos. There's no need to give the ego such negative connotations. Without an ego, we would not have our unique personality traits, characteristics, or preferences. The ego isn't at fault here; it's our lack of understanding of its true nature that is the issue. Wouldn't it be wonderful to fully understand the purpose of the ego? I believe we are missing a crucial piece of information about it. It would seem that ego becomes a distorted part of us and thus, the cause of all of humanity's problems and conflicts. This has been true throughout history. If that is truly the case, it implies that we lack something in this perfect piece of equipment. In my opinion, that's what body, mind, and soul are: the perfect devices through which to experience life.

The Projection of the Ego

Separation has its roots in the mechanisms of the ego. Once I understood and accepted this, it became easier to function; a continuous fight with the ego was futile. Until that time, my soul was overshadowed by the intense and distorted influence of my ego. When my perception of my ego changed and I began to understand its power, it became easier to manage and to align the roles of my ego, body, and soul with my real purposes and needs.

This is now clear to me, but for a long time I was confused by the contradictive information being presented. Initially, I was happy to be in my ego; it made perfect sense. When introduced to the notions that we are not our egos and that the ego is the root of all human problems, I became confused. It was a painful way of living because I no longer felt in control.

The awareness of separation from others starts at a very early age; we often spend the rest of our lives longing for unity. Unconsciously, we know we are one with others and the universe. If someone would've told me that separation is necessary, but not real, would I have believed it? Quite possibly. When we're young, we have a higher capability of grasping many concepts. Consider what occurred with a friend's three-year old daughter, Alba:

> Alba: "Mum, when are these voices going to stop?"
> Mum: "What voices?" The little one was not imagining
> things; she was just noticing her internal dialogue.
> Alba: "The voices inside my head."

I believe that if we really listen, we can gain valuable wisdom and insight from children. First, we have to come to an agreement as to what we're going to teach, and then find a natural, fun way to help them learn. Ideally, children would grow up understanding that, despite our individuality, we are indeed one, that division is natural, but that ultimately we're still all one. Perhaps we would suffer less in our daily encounters?

Ego is our identity—our individuality that makes us unique and different from others, but not special. When we start to feel *special*, we've fallen under an illusion. By definition, an illusion is a distortion of reality, usually involving the senses, including perception. Sooner or later, an illusion will bring us suffering in some form. We are not our bodies, our minds, our jobs, or the roles we play in life.

While studying social psychology, there was the argument that humans could be defined by the totality of their social roles. If that were the case, what happens to a man, for example, when he ceases to be a father, a lover, a boss, a successful painter, or any other role he temporarily undertakes? You know the answer: attachment to the role can only end with pain and suffering. This is why the ego's been portrayed as a negative force. Giving up the fight against specialness represents a release from a never-ending fight taking place in the mind.

Does this mean that I have no attachments? Of course not; it only means that I don't see them in a negative light, but examine them to see what's real, what I'm trying to obtain, and what it is that I think I need.

Ask yourself, "Why am I attached to this? What do I believe it offers me?" The ego is there to help experience whatever it is that is wanted or needed in life. Without it, we wouldn't be able to identify ourselves as separate beings with unique qualities and desires. The problem with this is that we in the West are relatively new to the concept of ego. Hence, we don't understand it well, nor do we use it correctly. The Eastern cultures have long been more aware of the role the ego plays in our lives and therefore, understand it better.

On a personal note, my understanding of self has evolved a little at a time with love and patience towards myself and others. This has made me aware of the games the ego plays 75 percent of the time. It allows me to enjoy my personality traits and develop them, which in turn, nourishes me and I have fun. It's not natural to fight against our uniqueness, to get caught up in the bad ego chase that can be just as bad as being trapped in the ego in the first place.

Find out what your unique traits are; live them to their full potential, but don't get attached to them. This is a life experience that we can all have. Initially, this happens sporadically, but little by little, we grow in other areas by observing ourselves, questioning ourselves, and especially by laughing at ourselves. For example, if you are close to someone, I suggest giving the ego of that person a different name. When you see it misbehave, you could say to the person kindly and tactfully, "I see Roberto is back today!"

You can also think of a little mind drama you recently experienced and have a good laugh at it. Try it; if you can do it with one, you will do it with two and then with three. Be prepared to laugh it up!

Analogy of the Chariot

When we try analytically to understand things with our minds that can't be understood through the logical process, we need to look inside. Our hearts always know what is true for us, the same way we know when we're in love or not. Our hearts own knowledge (intuition) and understanding. These shouldn't be overruled by the mind when we are attempting to make sense of the world. In fact, it's the heart's same wish to validate its own knowledge that's made great thinkers pursue their desire to create, invent, and study. Most of them reported what they considered to be an irrational drive, a knowing, intuition, gut feeling, or vision. In fact, the mind and the heart (along with the body) form the pathway to our internal worlds. The *I Ching* states that the master knows how to live with one foot in each world—one in the external, material world and the other in our internal world. If we combine the forces within our hearts and minds to understand the language of our emotions and feelings, we'll live more harmonious and richer lives.

We must enlarge our knowledge of the world in a way that supports the whole and incorporates the multidimensional characteristics of our lives. These must include our bodies, minds, and souls; all of these parts form the totality of the person we are (see Chapter 7). We're not just biological bodies creating thoughts, feelings, events, and experiences at random. Inside each of us is a unique desire(s) that agrees with the whole and is waiting to be expressed.

This chariot's analogy is explained in detail in the *Katha Upanishad* 1.3.3–9 where it discusses the nature of the human body.

This is the reason you are alive now. The first time I realized the importance of having teamwork on the inside of me was when I was introduced to the analogy of the chariot. It explains this concept and also provides powerful and easy visual imagery for the mind to retain. It compares a human being to a chariot and compares its parts as follows:

- The chariot represents the physical body.
- The horses represent the emotional body, which includes the five perception senses.
- The driver represents the intellect.
- The passenger represents the soul.

Most people can easily understand this. However, the issue arises when they are asked which part they think represents them? Most identify with the driver (the one in charge). The answer is that you are all of the parts, plus the passenger. Shortly after being told this, the people look lost, not because they do not see the logic, but because they have no idea how to communicate with their passenger who is representative of the soul.

Keeping this image in mind is a powerful reminder. There's a soul, a driving intelligence and a living force operating inside of us at levels that we're just now beginning to understand. Biologists have identified neuropeptides that correlate with each emotion we feel. These chemicals are also known to be at the root of our addictions and suffering. This analogy made reference to these desires and emotions as horses that need to be tamed in order to carry the chariot effectively. In the *Interview with Your Self* process, I'm able to gain clarity each time about what is driving my chariot: my emotions (horses), fear, desires, unquestioned thoughts, or my soul (passenger). Is my driver doing its job (intellect-ego), or has it fallen asleep under the illusion of specialness?

If we consider that life is an experience of the soul and it is also the passenger inside the chariot, we ultimately decide to relinquish control of what the soul knows is best for our fulfillment. The reason we have a problem identifying with the passenger is because the passenger isn't in the physical body as such.

Although I can't describe with certainty the whereabouts of the soul, I can share with you a concept that may help. To do this, I'll make use of another analogy. Imagine that you're watching a Robert Redford movie; the information is there, but Robert Redford isn't in the video. The video player is a device that contains the movie in what we can call a space-time event. That's what these so-called experiences are, space-time events, meaning that they occupy a location that has a beginning and an end. Everything is in a space-time location and always moving forward. This leaves our souls free of body and mind boundaries. Remember the phrase, "In the world, but not of it?" Your soul isn't attached to your body. Therefore, it isn't in a location of time and space; it's limitless. Are you beginning to see the implications of this? The decision maker is an infinite choice maker never limited by the chariot, nor by external circumstances or events.

It wasn't so long ago that I also believed that I was the *doer*; that I had to do everything in my life, or that others around me had to do things for me. I've come to understand the difference between spontaneous doing that is innocent of what you have reflected on doing or planned on doing for a particular reason. It took me some time and experience before I was clear on the difference intellectually and experientially. The challenge was in the practice and required more introspection. After a while, it becomes your true experience, a piece of information to build upon that you won't soon forget.

Your soul does everything for you if you will stop, put yourself aside, and let it come through.

When it does come through, the doors open and the people show up, along with the solutions in ways you would not have imagined. All of that wisdom and more resides inside of you. Remember, it's an organic process; by repetition you will be creating new pathways at a neuronal level. As a result, these will translate into new habits and new experiences. It will take some practice at first and may even seem a little overwhelming, but eventually it will become second nature. The benefits of making that effort are limitless.

How Can I Help?

Once you begin to understand how the ego speaks to you, you'll have opportunities to observe yourself as separate from it. You'll see it as a tool, rather than identify with it. Let's compare this experience to one of learning a new language. You must be patient, accept making a fool of yourself now and again, and be diligent in your practice. When you get your life in order and move into the real perception of life and its events, you contribute to the flux of all. You'll have a larger impact on those around you and on your immediate environment.

Whenever we learn new skills and concepts, we all benefit. Everyone's contribution, no matter how insignificant it may seem, is of vital importance to the evolution of all. It's now easier to grasp this concept because we see how the global village looks. We can understand better how the greed of a foreign president affects the whole, how religious beliefs in a foreign part of the world affect our daily lives, and how the exploitation of the resources in a faraway forest threatens our lives. This is the same principle, but it works at a micro level. Once you start making changes to your thinking patterns, you begin to view the world differently; you react differently, and as a result, others will react differently. They will be influenced to change how they see and do things, thereby impacting their environment positively.

I must stress a point here. Changing your thinking patterns and getting your body, mind, and soul in balance is *your* business. This doesn't extend to attempting to coerce others to get theirs in balance; that's *their* business. Relationships provide the only possibility for us to put these changes into practice. We start initially by applying changes to our personal lives, and then later, we extend these to our social and professional relationships. This is the natural flow and is how it happened for me. At first it was painful, especially since I didn't have all the tools and ideas that I have now. I had to endure an engaged battle with myself. I would like this book to help you avoid some part of the trial and error process. However, reading a book, alone, will still not do it; cultivating the practice of it will.

The interview process aims to identify patterns and provide clarity that's necessary for us to adjust our actions according to our new visions. The questions are designed for reflection and are asked in a manner that allows you to identify more quickly where you're coming from—your soul or your mind. This allows us to create new thought patterns that help blend input from both. For years, our egos have been the driving force in our lives; now it has to be just *a* force, not the driving one. That's why it's so important for us to learn the language of the soul and the language of the ego, and how these are uniquely expressed inside of us.

The ego is always operating and influencing you. While that's alright, it's necessary to control how far we allow it to go. Be sure that the ego's driving force is for the good of all. To make the distinction between the two, let's examine this further. Are you reverting to your old ways of assuming your specialness, or to your new way of understanding your uniqueness? Don't make a fuss about that either; remember, everyone is unique. It's important to maintain a good dose of humility and modesty; these will always be your best allies. You may find that you'll make this new endeavor your search for the *holy grail*. That is your ego starting its transformation; it has just changed its face. It will become easy to see as you bring it to the surface. The ego will tend to move you towards separation, but the soul moves towards union. The ego may attempt to alienate you one way or another. The best way to address this is to take life as it comes; you are not to push, but rather just to observe, cultivate, adapt, and correct the patterns that are showing up daily as resistance or blocks arising in your path. Spend some time every day practicing your newly found skills.

If we have a negative perception of someone or something, we can use the interview process to allow us to gain some insight and clarity about that situation. We then can make changes according to our new vision and understanding. There will be times when you already hold the correct vision and your questions only help you to get clear on your next course of action. This would be action more in line with your soul. There may be times when no action is necessary. It will require patience and receptiveness in order for life to guide you through the process and allow you the necessary space to create. In Ayurveda, space is the basic element; without it, nothing happens or exists.

Throughout the process I've learned that the language of my soul will always be patience, perseverance, allowing action or not if inappropriate, as well as receptiveness to life and others. The soul is always modest, humble, and needs no recognition from others. It is self-sufficient and true to self. This is all positive energy in contrast to the language of the mind or ego that can manifest as impatience, righteousness, and inappropriate action toward yourself or others. The ego is not open to the soul's input; its reference is external and its aim is the individualization process; its pursuit is to feel good. Because the ego's goal is to avoid pain and feel pleasure, it will make allowances for betrayal of yourself and others. These are important points to remember when you become confused. (There's more on this subject in the Interview in Chapter 6. See also Appendix II for more on emotions of body, mind, and soul.)

Enlightenment has been described as a higher state of consciousness that consists of looking at the world without the distorted visions and perceptions of the ego. It involves the transmuting of an intellectual or abstract concept into an experience of universal truth—from believing into being. Enlightened persons aren't involved in the pursuit of an altered state of consciousness. They are involved in the enlightenment of others without forcing and by just *being*. The ego can get in the way because it's usually involved with a dualistic, distorted vision of the self, others, and the world. One could say that the experience through the distorted perception of the ego is the altering of our consciousness.

We cannot afford to continue living in this state, as the price we pay as individuals and as a civilization is too high and creates too much suffering. Still, it's up to each of us to do something about it, starting with ourselves. We might not reach enlightenment, but we may observe enough to raise our awareness. Can you imagine a life free of worry, anxieties, stress, guilt, and anger? These are some of the benefits of cultivating a daily practice of self-examination. Nothing more is required than your consistency and patience.

Chapter 3

THE STORIES WE ARE TOLD

In this chapter we're going to take a little time to explore our stories as a race and as individuals. We need to be able to see through all the misconceptions and misunderstandings, both large and small.

We live in a society that feeds off of our fears and insecurities. We've been told what to do from the start, what religion to practice, what colleges are best, what we should study, and even what we should do to become successful. When we fail to accomplish these or any other social/cultural goals, we begin to feel like worthless failures. On the other hand, if we're lucky enough to succeed, we fall into the trap of "you need more" or "it is not good enough." You have a degree, but now you need a Masters; you are the sales executive, but now you need to be the director, and so on. It's the same thing in our personal lives; as soon as we become young adults, the pressure starts. We need to fit in, be attractive to the opposite sex, get married, and then have children. Just writing about this makes me feel part of the proverbial rat race.

The same applies to groups; as a family, we play a part in the scenario. We have to be the happy family, live in the right neighborhood, and keep up with the material possessions of our peers as if we're in a competition. Our egos expand the same way, from personal to family to local to national to religious. This seems to be the human condition. However, we may still feel that we're better (more special) than the rest of the animal kingdom. If you look at our history—the wars, depressions, hunger, violence, rape, murders—you'll see that we have mastered the skill of *specialness* at a very high price: the freedom of choice. It's about time that we started looking beyond our belly buttons and become focused on our progress at every level; we have what we have because we are what we are. Are we going to keep repeating the same stories again and again on the personal and global levels?

Working with others, I've observed that when a client was abused as a child, it's highly likely that the abuser was also abused. When it comes to families, we often see that parents try to change the patterns of abuse through succeeding generations. For example, it may go from a grandfather who practices corporal punishment to a father who has anger issues, and then to a child who may have gained better control over anger issues. To some degree, progress takes place as the evolution unfolds. The question is, can we snap out of this semi-conscious reality of repeating the negative experiences a little faster? We live in the age of communication. We have Internet, emails, and social networking that move so fast that it's hard to imagine the process could not be positively speeded up. We can plug into the new information, concepts, and ideas that allow us to get out of this meaningless way of existence and move forward for the good of all. How much longer are we going to hold on to our restrictive history and beliefs?

What's Your Story?

Our stories never end. What has happened to you that you need to move through? The reasons why you're in a particular situation can be found in your story. The memory bank of our inner self holds all of the answers to help us understand where we went wrong or not, what failed us and why, as well as how we can be restored and healed.

We need to look closely at the events and situations that happened in the past in order to use them as building blocks for who we want to be in the future. If we are still feeling wronged, we need to understand why we feel that way. The feelings of failure, wrongness, sadness, or any other negative emotion are what we need to make us see that we have separated ourselves from our Source. Anytime we allow the language of negative emotion into our lives, we feel pain, because these values are not true and are foreign to the way of nature. They are deceptive tricks taught to us by society. In any given moment, our feelings and emotions arise to get our attention so that we can revise them and release ourselves from their

21

negative influence. Once we're clear on what it is that's making us sick and unhappy, we come to see how it contradicts what we would like to be. We suddenly become motivated and are released from our *story*. Some of us have been carrying it around for years, but are now free to move on to the next stage of our lives. This is how using the *Interview with Your Self* repeatedly will help us gain clarity and get rid of that which no longer serves us. Personally, I'm happy to see all of these things go from my life.

It's imperative to assess where we're stuck, not only to know where we are, but where we intend to go. What is an accessible goal for some is only a dream for others because they don't believe they can reach it. We know that some dreams will never come true, such as having a magic wand that solves all of our problems. Therefore, we know that no effort should be put into chasing that specific dream. We also know that other dreams—working for one's self, having a family, or traveling around the world—could come true, but only if we believe in ourselves and move towards manifesting them.

It's only the brave ones (sometimes considered the *crazy ones*) who take the first step towards a goal and ultimately enter into the real wonder of life. When we look for inspiration, knowledge, and the expertise of people we admire people who achieved what we are trying to achieve, it's still important to remain true to our uniqueness and avoid stepping into someone else's story.

The majority of the media portrays what is commonly held as desirable. However, we must always be true to what is desirable, while remembering our individual self. For example, you might choose a new career that's well suited for others, but not for you. The same is true when you choose a path for personal development; it should be something that nourishes you and that touches you on a soul level. It cannot be because it's the newest fad or method in town, nor the oldest. You have to identify with what resonates *within* you. Although we always know, we still sometimes ignore this information and go for the fastest solution or the path of least resistance.

When it comes to the truth, no matter what twists and turns life takes, you will end up having to listen to your inner self, what some call your *gut feeling.* When looking for a spiritual practice, we should look for one that we enjoy, look forward to, and feel its benefits quickly. For example, someone who loves playing a piano would look into ways to perfect their practice, while enjoying the process. This is why I believe it would be best to eradicate the word *lesson* from the spirituality dictionary.

Although professionals tend to have a better understanding and respect for the uniqueness of the process, no one is in a position to offer you a proven map that will take you where you want to go. They can only share some of their light—a light that should place a spark in your heart and help you go inside of yourself to find your truth. In fact, you know deep down that life doesn't sustain those kinds of absolute systems, apart from the one that is the creation and destruction cycle of life or what some call the *circle of life*.

I have seen many spiritually aware and committed people suffer from guilt, failure, and other negative emotions. The reason is that they think they are not doing *it* by the book if they fail to make their daily affirmations, do their yoga every day, or even practice detachment to the extent they feel they should.

In finding your own particular path, never confuse the path with the goal. We are making it all up as we go. The river of life just moves even faster when we go with the flow and don't struggle; it will take us to where we need to go eventually. We can differ in our methods and there is nothing wrong with that. For me, a good way to validate what I do is by interviewing myself. Examples:

—Am I enjoying my path?
—Do I look forward to my practice every day?
—How often do I do it?
—Do I lose track of time while doing it?
—Was it so enjoyable that when I finish, do I wish I could continue?
—Is it progressing little by little into other areas of my life?

These are questions that will help you find your unique path, whether it's by practicing yoga, Zen, or Interviewing Your Self. It may be another method you choose to use, such as writing, painting, walking, or fishing. The common denominators on the results should be:

—Are you a happier person?
—Is this reflected in the way you relate to others?

—Is it reflected in the way you live?

—Are you feeling connected to a higher source?

If you really want to materialize your dreams, there are many tools you can employ to help you reach your creative potential. Anything that feels truly authentic to you will be supportive of the whole; the vision of our higher self is always that of union with the cosmos, with God. Therefore, any assistance you get from others should be classified as inspirational, enlightening, and even challenging.

If you use the process of creation explained in the next chapter, you will be able to find what it is that you want. You also need to know where you want to go, and then become acutely aware of your motivation. The important point here is that you need to move in the direction that feels best to you, one that expands your unique gifts and talents in a natural manner in accordance with your vision.

By talking to family, friends, or even experts in a field of interest, we can pick up hints as to what's in our way, what's in our best interest, what's positively on our side, what personal traits most benefit us, and where we need improvement. This approach is like seeing the journey in our internal GPS and thinking ahead. It tells us the fastest way to get from where we are to where we want to go. Having goals is imperative; having learning tools is also important, but knowing how to use them and where we are in the journey are vital.

"Traveler, the road is only
your footprint, and no more;
Traveler, there is no road
The road is your traveling."

—Antonio Machado, from *Cantares (Songs from Machado's Testament)*

Remember to consider that things might not always turn out as we planned. Revisions to our journey are acceptable and necessary. It's about our readiness and willingness to accept change. By taking this approach, it means that you enter into a frame of mind that sees diversions on the path as relevant opportunities for the journey. This is very important so that we don't get distracted, confused, or disheartened and abandon our goal altogether.

Let's use the analogy of your GPS. It can provide you with many routes from point A to destination B. Consider that you might find excess traffic, run out of gas, take the wrong turn because of a distraction, or find a road blocked. These and many other events may be completely out of your control. Although any of these might create initial resistance in you, none of them is a good enough reason to give up your cherished trip. You might eventually see how important it is for you not to be on that bus, in that meeting, or whatever you missed. In retrospect, you can easily identify that it was really the best outcome for all concerned. Once you learn to identify and pay attention to the coincidences (obviously, there *are* no coincidences), you learn about synchronicity and how important it is to trust whatever life brings to you. That's a challenge and a sign of your own mastery. Therefore, it's important to see clearly and to give yourself the credit you deserve, having been able to embrace a situation with acceptance and humility.

Our Story So Far

It's not my intent to discuss theology at length, but nevertheless, in a book that considers the human being to be made up of body, mind, and soul, there must be some consideration given to what God and religion are.

I grew up as a Roman Catholic and attended a college operated by nuns. At one stage of my life I thought about becoming a nun. I loved the church and the singing at Mass. By the age of thirty-two, I had a long list of arguments with friends about the validity of the Scriptures and religious beliefs, despite the fact that I had not read much of the Bible in years. I sometimes became irrational, but I didn't understand why. What made me do this? By that time, I had long since stopped attending church regularly.

In retrospect I realize I was afraid, very afraid to feel the empty space that my lack of spiritual practice and understanding was creating. It was an internal abyss, full of questions that I didn't want to investigate. I was using my religious upbringing as a Band-Aid, but it didn't heal my pain. I was like many people: a believer without belonging, connection, or a practice. The family gatherings at church for Christmas and other celebrations were a big guilt trip for me, especially not having been to the required confession or communion in years, which made me feel ashamed of myself.

I didn't allow this to stop me. After some difficult experiences I started to investigate the power of positive thinking, not just because I wanted to have more of that power, but because I have always been positive. I could relate to that quality, but didn't know how I could ever relate to a God up in the sky. I had a strong conviction that Jesus was an authentic, great human being when he was in human form, so I felt more inspired by him. Still, that had no great impact on my day-to-day experience.

Despite all of this confusion, I was strongly attached to the beliefs about God and the world that I was brought up with. At times, I even felt the need to defend those ideas. Back then my mind and soul were in two different realities. My mind was in the material world; my soul was in the after- or spiritual world. I was a rational person, or at least that was what I thought; but somehow, nothing made much sense.

It was on a flight from London to Peru that I talked to a young man sitting next to me on the plane. After a nice long conversation on positive thinking and human behavior, the young man gave me a book called *Tomorrow's God* by Neale Donald Walsch. It was the first time I felt that a book spoke to my soul, as well as to my mind; it just made perfect sense. I was so fascinated that I read more and more on the material presented in the *Conversations with God* series. To this day, I've benefited by this new way of approaching our spirituality because the new paradigm empowers us both individually and collectively.

Since then my ideas about God have never been the same. It was a fresh start for me; what came after changed my experience of God progressively and dramatically. I realized that I really didn't know much about God, at least the real God that I was coming to believe in. Perhaps you're one of those who, just like me, didn't know where to look for answers. There are too many people on the planet going through their life not comprehending, let alone paying any attention to, their souls. You will notice that I refer to names like the Source, Tao, Cosmos, the Divine, Universal Force, or Life Intelligence when I refer to God in this book. That's because for me God is each of those things and all of them at once by whatever name you prefer to use. I do not want to be trapped by a particular definition of God; I am more interested in the *experience* of God. This might also help the reader to consider the limitations and implications of our language. Because I don't want the reader to be put off by any one word, I may change the words I use to refer to the Divine.

I have recently observed a trend in people who, like me, have become disenchanted with the Western approach to the Creator; many are now showing an interest in the ideologies of the East in contrast to many of the organized religions of the West. Unfortunately many, if not most followers do not really understand their religion or study it in-depth. It's the same with many of the Abrahamic religions (main religions that descend from the Abraham traditions, including Islam). Although it's good for people to have more options, we still don't fully understand any of them. In fact, most religious people are busy defending their beliefs out of fear, and from my experience, that's not a fun place to be.

It's true that our ideas and fears about God are behind all of our problems. My focus of concern here is to have you examine how your concepts of God affect your everyday life. I will briefly mention some of the concepts that are creating confusion, and in some cases, much suffering. For this purpose, let's look separately at the religions of the West and some of the ways they differ from those of the East.

Western religions contain contradictory concepts that are in direct opposition to science; that has created skeptics. We've made substantial progress in the scientific fields, but there's great difficulty in coupling this progress with religion. Scientology was founded to address this issue and is mostly made up of a mixture of Eastern concepts and practices. Western ones of similar line of thought are often touted as Gnostics and Illuminati. Here we wish to avoid debate and avoid reinforcing the idea of a demanding or punishing God, as well as the concepts of demons and evil. This is a matter of individual perception.

So what is the purpose of religion? Is it to weaken us or to empower us? Is it to unite us or divide us? Does it even make good sense for one religion or belief system to claim that it has the *only* truth? The knowledge that something was wrong with this picture made me search for the perfect explanation and the authentic response, along with the practices to attain union/communion with the Divine. I found that there are many paths to what we seek. It's important to approach any religion with an open mind and remain neutral. In the words of many other authors, take what speaks to you and leave what does not, but be especially careful with the concepts that fragment or disempower you.

I've observed specific concepts that have affected me, as well as my clients: dualistic concepts of good v. bad and sin v. saintly; they place things either here or there. It is better to look at things as if they were in motion rather than in black or white terms. Duality is okay, but we forget the *between* area that is the gray in the middle. The ego also gets in the way; it operates within society. We are different from each other; so are the various races, nationalities, and customs. The more one travels, the more one will find diversity to be enchanting and wonderful. Uniformity isn't a natural concept; it's imposed on us by structures and systems. Remember that when we start to feel special and that we are the chosen ones, we are entering the territory of a mind distortion. Most Western religions fail in the sense that they consider God to be an external being outside of oneself who demands that we be and act in a certain way and who will only love us if we do as we are commanded. They don't consider that humans have frailties, such as fear, guilt, confusion, incompetence, or ignorance. These frailties, they believe, can even result in a soul falling short of the mark, thereby deserving eternal punishment. Some religions teach that we need this *Law and Order* God because we can't be trusted due to our original sin. How can we, as humans, enjoy a relationship with a God who's always in a bad mood? (for more I recommend you read Conversations with God I) by Neale D. Walsh

The Eastern traditions don't have all of the answers either. Some of their concepts better explain God's love and they hold a more gentle approach to life. Hinduism, Taoism, and Buddhism all agree on the concept that we all live under an illusion (*Maya*) of ignorance and that only when we overcome this ignorance will we reach enlightenment (Moksha, Tao, Nirvana).But because the veil of ignorance is so strong, we continue to reincarnate.

In Hinduism, God is fragmented and all souls are under the illusion of the ego (Maya) that must be transcended in order to attain liberation. The souls have to undergo a series of lessons through painful experiences in the cycle of birth, life, death, and rebirth (reincarnation) until they achieve Moksha. Tao and Buddhism also share the karma and reincarnation beliefs. Karma in these terms (and for most of the general population) is understood as basically the accumulation of bad deeds done in previous lives and that we are required to clear in order to reach liberation. Karma is a large flowing pattern of action and reaction. It involves and intertwines one life with another; it's much larger than we can ever imagine and is related to one's unique qualities and the archetypical dynamics of the psyche. To be able to understand the concept of karma, one must be able to transcend the *existence* dimension of life and move into the *nonexistence*. The details are so large that it is only from this nonexistential space outside of us that we can begin to glimpse the concept and patterns of karma.

Karma is like an inherited birth-mark or the freckles on your face. So many karmic patterns are involved—each playing a different part in our lives—that it's sometimes difficult to ascertain their source. Karma is not a bookkeeping log of good and bad actions that determine the path your life will take. Karma is a platform of unique patterns forming the tools you are equipped with to help your soul rise to a higher level. The patterns hidden in our karma are so extensive that they encompass our DNA, the psychological patterns of the psyche, as well as the way we express our souls in this and other lives. They comprise the mechanics by which we write our personal profile, our individual and physical existence. A worm that has no concept of his future as a butterfly undergoes the metamorphosis without choice; it's encoded in its DNA. We are the same. None of us is less than a wonderful butterfly with its unique size and colors. And like the worm, not one of us will be able to avoid his or her destination. We can find responses to all of our questions in the repetitive cycles of nature.

Nevertheless, our minds' logical process has a need to search for complex responses; we feel the need to reject simplicity, yet simplicity is full of wisdom.

Closer examination reveals that most Eastern religions and Western belief systems have a similar concept: they place God outside of us, as if God were an external being somewhere in the universe. They all agree that humans suffer from delusions or sins; these need to be overcome in order to end suffering. Life everywhere seems to be a school full of hard, difficult, painful lessons that one must master in order to become free. What are we hoping to become free of—life itself?

These beliefs all create ideas of struggle, failure, pain and suffering. to one degree or another. What is the real point to life then? If we aim to reach liberation and avoid the deceptions of this world, why not start there?

This would make it appear that either almighty God is really mean or not so almighty. While we have no proof of certain concepts, does it even make sense that we were created to suffer because we are human? It's our thoughts about these concepts that create suffering. Somehow, it doesn't ring true that this is how it is meant to be.

All religions maintain that the goal is to achieve union with the Divine. However, this implies that we're separated from the Divine (even if through delusion). Hence, it is a long way back home for most of us because we're starting the journey with misleading information.

Finding that I am one with the Divine—no matter what— is an experience no one will ever take from me. I may become confused when my old programmed beliefs and habits make me lose sight of this fact. That's precisely why I enjoy my practice so much; it's my going home to God.

To learn more about understanding yourself and God, I would recommend reading and studying *What God Wants,* by Neale Donald Walsch.

Mediation is the path, not the destination; the destination is freedom and happiness. The same can be said about religion.

I invite you to open yourself completely in body, mind, and soul. Be open to the human experience; search, question, contradict yourself, play, and have fun. Life isn't meant to be so serious.

You may, however, choose another option: no God, no religion, and no soul-searching or a still incomplete material and scientific approach. However, be attentive so that you don't end up living as if you were never going to die, and later die as if you had never lived. Unfortunately, that's what many people end up doing. It's as complicated or as simple as we wish to make it. Observation alone will tell you that life's intelligence goes far beyond our limited perceptions. Merely looking at ourselves in the mirror will help us to understand the wonders of our bodies' structures, as well as the intelligent systems of nature through its wonderful forms.

They gather together by the sea, many all so different and happy people. They tell stories; the stories they use to believe of times long ago, when people were fearful of God, fearful of life.

Chapter 4

THE PROCESS OF CREATION

Your Creative Process

When everything is going well in our lives, we have an intense sense of well-being. Our bodies feel lighter, we have unlimited energy, we're optimistic, we have a good and loving attitude towards others, and we experience an extraordinary feeling of connection to the world, nature, and everything that surrounds us. We become open to the nonexistence, and we're happy *with* existence. The flow of *Chi* goes through our bodies and connects us to nature's flow and to others. It handles each situation without any conflict or resistance. Don't we want to feel like that all of the time?

The main focus of this chapter is how we block our flow and how we get back into going with the flow. The process of creation has been debated for centuries by diverse cultures in relation to the power of positive thinking, the power of intention, and the law of attraction. The topic isn't that clean-cut; there is a nonmaterial element. In order to create with it, we need to understand it; for some of us that will mean we need further information. The world of paradox and uncertainty has a big impact on our lives and at times, can leave us feeling powerless. It's comforting to know that all the power is and always has been inside of us. It's through persistence, endurance, and inner power that we will thrive.

I've always felt that I was a person with the power to control my life. Once, I embarked on a long journey across the ocean, only to find that I had little power over the tides and the winds. What a shock that was to me. I realized that I really was powerless in certain situations and I suddenly became very afraid. It is the same with life when storms arrive. For example, I recall my feelings of frustration and sadness when I closed down my well-being center. I'd invested so much time, strength, love, and money and still could not control the twist the financial world took in 2008. Little did I know to what extent life (as I knew it) was going to change and how everyone would be affected to some degree or another. What was going on? I had done all of the right things, so where were my results? I wanted to pick the fruits of my labor. When was I going to get a break? Sound familiar? The resistance started to surface, and by that time, they were stronger than ever before.

I talk of tides and winds, but as you can see, it's not a fairy tale. It's life itself throwing us adversity and we have to deal with it. When this happens over a long period of time, it's easy to lose faith and abandon our good habits and intentions. We find ourselves in the middle of the ocean where it's lonely and very scary at times. In fact, all of our personal resistances grow stronger during tough times because then we feel exposed. It's as if life seduces us into following it and then suddenly, out of the blue, everything disappears into thin air.

Those of us who are adventurous risk takers feel the need to be enticed to embark on a new project, job, career, or relationship. It's this new situation that moves us out of our comfort zone. Others may have to be forced—people who dislike change and prefer the familiar. Often, a major challenge outside of their comfort zone forces them to make needed changes. One way or another, each of us—the rich, the poor, the good person who always did as he was told and the one who never did—has to experience continuous challenges in life. The creative process is composed of extension and contraction, day and night, storm and calm. All of these opposites are necessary for the creation of the perfect situation by way of its deterioration into a chaotic situation and its reassembling into a new, perfect situation.

The problem for some of us is that we feel we have some control, but then find out we don't. For others, it may be that they had a long-term plan for themselves and went by the book. Then things did not go according to their plans. We forget to allow for the twists and turns of life or even consider the nature of life, the nature of change, and the reasons for adversity. Sometimes we're faced with adversity simply because we are not looking at the given situation correctly; we are either too fixed on our goal (considering only one possible type of outcome), or we have expectations as to how the journey should unfold. We fail to see when, despite the fact that things are not going as we wish, we can still make the necessary adjustments. It's certainly possible for us to use the winds and tides in our favor if we can simply stop reacting to them. Like everything else in life, we always have a solution inside us.

A new scenario challenges us by forcing us to make changes to the course. It makes us change our minds about something or find something else. This is a process called *creativity*. Humans have a master's degree in this precise process, but aren't fully aware of it. Our emotional, addictive behaviors are in the way 95 percent of the time. When we get too comfortable and attached to the things we know, we stop being creative or innovative and relax. Nothing's wrong with that, but we forget that everything is changing all of the time and that change is all there is.

When we are in a new situation at sea, or in the middle of a perfect storm challenging us to our limits, we have the necessary coping tools, but they may not seem to be doing us any good at the moment. It is usually because we are not using them properly. If we are attached to things manifesting in a certain way, our reaction and responses are predictable; they are also based on information from the past.

Whether from the past, the environment, or our story, this information isn't necessarily relevant to what is happening right now. We try many things until we're forced to give up each one of our old tricks because none of them is working. We get so involved in our story that we forget all about the power of the nonphysical realm of existence of which we know so little. The truth is that there is no reason to despair; humans have lived millions of years with fewer tools than we possess. They always managed to find a new way. We will also, but we need to be open and receptive to the creative process.

The first and most difficult step is to give up the fight, the doing, the resistance blocking our connection to our higher self—the self that has a direct connection to the nonphysical side of our being. Why do we have trouble with this? Perhaps it's because we listen to the internal voices and follow their advice. They tell us we need to do something now, that the present situation cannot continue. These are all different forms of resistance interfering with our ability to reach clarity. Before we know it, we're in a spiral of emotions and programmed responses that engage our mind and body, making it more and more difficult to receive directions from the passenger inside the chariot. Our addictive behaviors come into full display and we're in automatic mode at a time that is full of potential for us. We're like a junky trying to get a quick fix.

Even if we appear to find that fix, most of the time, we fail to remember the difference between a quick fix and a genuine solution to the issue we face. A genuine solution requires going with the flow and it provides benefits for everyone involved. This may come as a signal of well-being in the body when breathing returns to normal and we're moving without restrictions, even though the issue at hand my not yet be resolved.

On the contrary, a quick fix doesn't normally work for an extended period of time because it isn't what we're really searching for. Often, it serves only to temporarily alleviate our fears and take us back into our comfort zone. It offers only a short-lived sense of relief and differs in its quality. There is an inner knowing that the problems still aren't resolved, so we remain alert and worried.

When we settle for less than what we desire just to survive, we're not being authentic or true to ourselves. Such patterns appear frequently in our lives. One example of this is when we allow or tolerate certain less than desirable behaviors in our children, partners, or work colleagues. It seems to be a quick fix for the relationships, but deep down, we know that's not who we really are. It's the same with matters of vocation; most of us settle for jobs that give us less than what we feel we deserve. They provide us with a false sense of security. All of these fixes might work for a given period of time, but not for the long term, because they deny and subjugate who we really are. We're not flowing with the river of life; but are holding a distorted vision of the river that now looks more like a reservoir.

We can also deny our truth by giving into our addictive patterns of behaviors. While we're doing this, we forget that the forces of life (*prana* and *chi*) are interrupted and we're no longer in balance at the body, mind, and soul level. We forget of what we're made and of what we are capable.

In the wise words of my own father, "A captain knows how to navigate the ship; you know how to navigate yours. In fact, you are the only one that knows how to navigate it and where you want to go." We just need to hold space in our daily lives in order to keep us in tune with our truths and let go of the mental clutter accumulated in our daily dealings with the external world. We forget, because for years, we've seen the world in a way that was foreign to our truth and; reinforced by our everyday surroundings. We need to allow things to become second nature to us, continuously reminding and reinforcing ourselves about what we know to be true.

The interview process will allow you to remind yourself often. I'm reminded on a daily basis of my true identity and my capabilities. All I need to do is take time to remember and reconsider what's happening. We must seriously make an effort to counterbalance the programming we absorb from society. This includes interacting with family, friends, colleagues, and others or even watching TV. First, get clear and ask your inner self three basic questions. Your answers will show you the way to deal with the direction the tides and winds of life take you. Allow yourself to use these forces to reach your destination.

The Most Important Questions

What is the purpose(s) of our lives? We've been told to study hard in order to get a good job, get married, have children, and enjoy all of the good things life has to offer. Is that all this is about? Or is there something else for you? To become clear, you need to answer these questions: Who am I? Where am I? What do I want?

How do we find our answers? Read. Many books offer different perspectives; no one book has all the answers. Take what rings true to you and leave the rest. In your search for answers, you might initially decide you want to be an artist, a lawyer, a mother, a teacher, or a businessman. Is it what you feel in your heart, or is it what someone has said you should be? With time, we lose identification with our social roles. Even when we are on a spiritual path, we fall prey to other stereotypes, such as the yogi, devotee, guru, wise man or woman, clairvoyant, or priest.

No matter what the belief system, we're ultimately the ones who must respond to questions, fill in the blanks, and move forward. This is because you—and you alone—are the only one who *can* respond to them. You're also the only one who gives meaning to your life. Remember, you're creating all of the time; even by just stopping, observing, and meditating, you affect your environment. Being loyal to self is the only viable way. How do you do that? By coming from body, mind, and soul. The mind and soul affect things at a level that isn't easy to see.

It isn't only normal, but it is necessary to take time to ponder these questions; do not rush the process. It's important to allow the responses to come to you in God's perfect timing. By now you have, no doubt, come to accept your spiritual nature. We are unlimited souls having a human experience. Isn't that more fun than just being a body having physical experiences? Earth is merely the stage for the roles we play while in our physical experience. Remember that we are not separate beings, but a part of the human network. We can play a large or small role, whether on the main stage or behind the scenes. Each one of us matters. Therefore, examine your inner self to find out how you can be of service. What are you passionate about? Are your talents specific to a cause? What activities are you so excited about that they make you lose track of time? Lastly, remember to allow for the responses to change because change is constant in the river of life.

During moments when we find ourselves in a sea of intense turmoil, our internal chatter can go something like this: "It's not fair! Why is this happening to me?" It's important to replace these questions by more empowering ones, such as, "Why do I think this is happening? How can I change what appears to be a negative event into a positive one in order to be who I really am? What do I want to be now in light of this new turn of events? What good can come from it?" This is empowering internal talk; not only will it help you to feel better, but you'll gain new clarity.

The process of creation can be very simple or very complicated. Be true to self. Don't look to others for answers; they are an internal experience. It is through these experiences (including trial and error) that we evolve. Again, there's no magic wand, but there are plenty of surprises ahead for you if you can stop thinking of them as threatening and remain open and neutral. Here is an exercise that can help:

Exercise 1:
Keep a journal handy at all times. Consider a situation you want to inquire about (work, finances, love, health, etc.). If you have no particular question in mind, just be open to guidance.

Imagine you have everything you want. You no longer think of people, events, or things as frightening. Instead, you've replaced fear with feelings of wonderment, curiosity, and excitement. Close your eyes and imagine experiencing them. How would they feel? Where in the body would you feel these? With your eyes still closed, observe your breathing to a count of eight breaths; then open your eyes and respond.

Write in your journal your response to the following questions. Make note of what you are feeling about the situation.

—What are your options?
—What feelings arose?
—What do you choose to be next?

An adequate response may also be to do nothing, especially if you had a strong desire to take action or wanted to reach a quick conclusion by avoiding a hasty decision. This is a powerful tool for gaining clarity. In order to empower yourself, you need to remember who you are, where you are, and where you want to go. Make sure that these realizations match what you're attempting to create. Does it match with what you're doing most of your time? If not, what can you do to change that?

Nothing is absolutely defined. Some of us have situations we can't fix, such as losing a limb or even a loved one. These losses are very painful and we must go through the pain of the grieving process. Be very kind and supportive of yourself; each one of us is needed to help the whole. When something can't be changed, the part of us that sees it as a problem can be changed. With guidance and self-love, we will heal and eventually see the situation differently.

I once suffered from a long-term illness. I did so in silence with no support from my family; they were far away from me and there was nothing they could do to help. The few friends I had around me at times didn't know how to relate. I decided that it was best for me to handle the illness on my own, to use it as a growth experience. I needed to keep calm, remain centered, and stay focused. I took the time to nurture myself to the best of my ability. It was a very hard period of my life, but I learned that I had more strength and more resources available than I had thought.

Questioning ourselves allows us to unfold new perspectives, even regarding events that can't be changed. If we open our minds to questions and then listen to the guidance of our souls, we can create and cocreate our realities. But we must consciously be aware of what it is that we *intend* to create. Although it's no one else's business what we intend to create, we must consider how it will affect others, the immediate environment, and even in some cases, the global community. For example, what can we do to get what we need and at the same time keep our environment and others around us in balance? The answer is *by always looking for the best solution for all involved.* By doing so, we're moving away from the concept of individuality and into a web of networking. If we want the world to be a kinder, gentler, and nurturing place for all forms of life, we can't neglect our power and input. When we decide to make this our first priority, we'll be in a better position to overcome personal and social issues and challenges we face.

There are times when we need to put ourselves and/or our family first. However, this is not the case in most of our daily experiences, although we sometimes act as if it were. Competitive attitudes pervade our work, personal relationships, and financial situations. If you're unhappy with the job or the people who surround you, find a more nourishing environment. This type of discontent is actually doing you a favor by making it clear to you that you can be happier elsewhere. It's amazing that when we finally make a decision, the universe conspires to help us recognize our creativity, build our confidence, and make us strong believers in ourselves.

Our current world is governed by a few people who have all the resources; that leaves most of us trying our entire lives to obtain what we're led to believe we should want. Before we realize it, much of our energy and resources have been spent on struggle, sacrifice, and hard work.

There's much we can do to help each other. We could help clean our waters, insist on new, greener cars on the road, recycle on a larger scale, and assist third world countries. The list really is endless. If we all did our part, the financial crisis would end. Even if we just stopped the continual attempt to revive a dead body of structures, instead of taking the next small step in front of us, things would change dramatically. Whether we like it or not, when we resist the flow, the river will rule. This is truly a time of opportunity.

The Nature of Thoughts

In the Eastern concept, thoughts are seen as energies that come and go (just like the clouds in the sky). We have as many as 60,000 thoughts passing our mental space every day. The person connected to the Tao sees them as separate entities, as products of the intellect and the ego and doesn't identify with them. That's easier said than done. Maybe we can at least stop identifying with most of them by starting with the ones that are doing real damage in our lives.

When a thought enters our mind's consciousness, we need to validate that thought. Thoughts tend to come to us by association; this is something that one can observe during meditation. For example, a thought comes that says, "It's so late and the children are not back yet." Then another follows, "How disobedient they are about timing." And yet another one follows, "They don't respect me or my authority." It continues to, "They could've gotten in the wrong car." The thinking process continues to distort until our peace of mind is destroyed. We play out in our minds all the possible negative scenarios until we feel them in our bodies. It's no exaggeration to say that this is a common occurrence for many parents when children are starting to venture out by themselves at night. It can create a lot friction, pain, and suffering in the family's relationship.

Because this association takes place in a very subtle manner, we don't clearly see the mechanism operating. An unconscious thought enters our mind and settles there, simply because we haven't questioned its validity. It has entered our unconsciousness and our bodies believes it to be true; therefore, it responds to it as if it's valid and real.

Here is another example: Suppose that I want my husband to give me more affection in the form of hugs and kisses. Moreover, I've been wishing this for years, but so far it hasn't happened. I'm not aware of the effect of this thought in our relationship. Hence, the thought that he should be more affectionate or attentive towards me will affect our relationship because it has become an unconscious thought.

Instead, I could invite myself to ask what he does do that I like and have always liked. How can I help him? I could try being affectionate whenever I miss it, instead of waiting for him to act. There are many other things we might do if we take the time to ponder, instead of going in circles.

The goal of this book is to discover how these thoughts are affecting our lives by creating unwanted feelings and reactions in our bodies towards ourselves or others. We respond to what we fear so quickly that most of the time we only see what really happened in hindsight. Reflection is good, but it would be less painful if we could be more neutral with our thoughts and allow them to come and go without getting attached. It takes practice to stop negative thinking. That's why questioning and writing thoughts down on paper can bring the clarity necessary to allow us to move into that innocent space inside of us. This space is full of neutrality and compassion for ourselves and others. Best of all, it's fully accessible.

As you write answers to your questions, you'll notice how we all have felt like a victim to some degree and have the same blurred vision of our day-to-day thoughts. Sometimes our thoughts can become so distorted and removed from reality that they become threats. If we allow these bombs to shatter our realities, we'll have a lot of work to do later trying to repair the damage. Therefore, it is crucial that we get clear and remove confusion by putting down answers to our questions on paper.

Another way to explore these thoughts is through meditation. You can also use a mixture of the *Interview with Your Self* process, the *I Ching* reading, and a combination of bodywork and meditation. This is especially effective with old, programmed thinking patterns. These techniques help us to become aware of the mechanics we are unconsciously using. Changes to the psyche are always a gradual, organic process. Therefore, regular practice is necessary in order to investigate our feelings and emotions every time we feel we've lost connection with our true selves.

Neuroscience has proven that our neuronal responses can be changed, just as our thoughts can be changed. Our thoughts stimulate our brain chemistry, creating our behaviors and our actions. Sometimes we're so focused on something that our responses are in automatic mode.

Most of us are doing our best with what we remember and understand at any given moment in time. This happens even to expert scientists in different fields. They discover a new law or concept, and then shortly, there appears another one to either reinforce or contradict it completely. Be patient with yourself and others; there's no such thing as *perfect*. You will constantly forget, but you'll have the opportunity to remind yourself again and again. In time you'll reach a point when it all becomes fun. Putting things down on paper offers us a wider perspective on our lives.

Chapter 5

GET IN TOUCH WITH YOUR ESSENCE

Life is information and energy formed by the consciousness of experience in a given location at a given moment in time. You can never become disconnected from your essence, because it's always there; you are surrounded by essence.

The *I Ching* talks about the image of the fish in a pond that suddenly changes direction. It's similar to a vision of us all swimming together and being guided by the essence, as fish or a flock of birds in the sky are experiencing unity and what is known as synchronicity.

Our essence is everywhere; we just don't experience it like that because our understanding of life and the soul is limited by our physical senses. Essence, the real you, is always connected. The question then is why do we seem to lose touch with our essence? It's because we've been taught to believe that all that exists is the world of *form*. The material world has taken control of our lives as evidenced by our habitual actions. We can surely reverse this if/when we recognize the source of the problem.

This doesn't mean that you're responsible for everything that happens to you, but you're responsible for a large percentage of it. As illustrates the example (see appendix IV) is the example of how a person answers the interview questions reveals a pattern. The person doing the interview understands that, although he is not directly involved with the corruption in the government, he unknowingly plays a part in it. He realizes that his lack of interest in politics (along with the rest of the population) has unwillingly contributed to society's problems. If the vast majority of citizens in a country exhibit that attitude, they're giving free reign to politicians to do as they wish. We tolerate injustices inflicted on both humanity and nature because we lack social involvement in the dynamics of society. We thus allow the proliferation of these events. It's my intention for all of us to become more aware so that we think and act in such a way as to responsibly cocreate more of what we want.

It's important that we not become distracted or rationalize our behaviors to the point of having excuses for everything that overwhelms us. We must be honest and make a sincere effort to be true to ourselves on all levels. The *Interview with Your Self* will help you to see how your internal world is indeed creating your external world.

The Importance of the Nonmaterial

We've been told that the material world is what's real and what matters. Some people believe that when they die, it's over. We don't remember previous lives, nor do we usually hold memories of our birth. We don't deny the later, not because we have memories, but because we have evidence in the testimonies of family members that we were born. What if we did not have these? Would we still agree that we were born on a specific day?

The *Tao* warns against this tendency to identify with only the material world. It points out that it's dangerous to consider what we see in the material world as real. The *Tao* states that reality is both the material and the nonmaterial and that neither of the two parts is more important than the other. This is not to imply that you don't need material things. After all, if you are hungry, you look for food. However, if we place too much emphasis on the nonphysical, it's taking things to the other extreme. We must always remember to avoid extremes, and to be sure to consider the whole.

Because we don't remember anything prior to our birth, we take it for granted that the only thing that counts is *this* reality, or what we can see in the material world. Have you ever wondered where you were before you were born and what will happen to you when you pass from this world? Of course, like me, you've questioned your immortality. Why would we want to be here forever anyway? Perhaps for a little holiday and then make a fresh start with a new form/body. Neglecting the spiritual (nonmaterial) dimension of life doesn't benefit us. Human consciousness and intelligence comprehend only the world we see; spirituality—the awareness of our nonexistence—should also be part of our daily lives. It doesn't matter now if you even believe in reincarnation. It's important to enjoy life while improving your experience.

Still find that difficult? Well just imagine this: Have you ever seen a thought? How can I see my thoughts? They materialize on paper and in my actions. I infer that I have thoughts from what I see they do in my life.

Now try the same with the nonphysical level of your being. I strongly urge you to commit yourself to the following exercise for a three-week period of time.

Perhaps before your meditation in the morning take your journal and write down a question to the universe—something related to your day ahead. Leave a blank space for the response. Take your journal with you so that you can make notes as you allow the response to come to you. Don't hold any expectation, but just ask and then journal the response when you receive it. You can ask anything, like "How can I be more understanding with my partner? How can I get the work done faster today? How am I going to deal with this problem?" It is likely that you'll get responses to your questions throughout the day, but don't be too disappointed if this doesn't happen. Don't attempt to get global responses to the questions; remember, life is an organic process and as such, things develop at the speed they should—not faster or slower. Normally you'll get a response, or at least a partial response, on the same day. However, it may not come in the form you expected. Be open to any type of response: an unexpected call, an understanding, a solution to a problem, unexpected help, or whatever form it takes.

This is because the spiritual/nonphysical existence is the storage facility for all that you know to be the truth. If you connect to it on a daily basis, you'll be plugging into the largest network of information and truth available to you. Your connection to your inner source will ultimately be the knowledge and wisdom from which you'll extract your unique ideas, visions, responses, and understanding. This wisdom will provide nourishment to your soul and assist you in connecting to your receptiveness, your inner voice, and your intuition. Insights will start to cocreate with your mind and body. This is how we create the space for it to come through as we learn to connect to our souls.

Another way to connect with our souls is by practicing the auto correction of difficult patterns of thoughts that keep us stuck. This is why it's important to regularly use the *Interview* process. It's also why I recommend that you do it for three weeks nonstop initially; in fact, the longer the better. Even though you may feel fine and think you no longer need to practice it, the process will help you to get clear on issues that keep you clinging to outworn, useless ideas, solutions, and concepts.

A suggested method of study might be to re-read and reflect on the following sections in this book:

Monday: Chapter 1 on Adversity
Tuesday: Chapter 1 on Change
Wednesday: Chapter 2 on Ego
Thursday: Chapter 2 on How I Can Help
Friday: Chapter 4 on Creation
Saturday: Chapter 5 on Essence
Sunday: Chapter 5 on Being v. Doing

Also important is the daily practice of meditation; sitting in silence with your spine straight for a minimum of twenty minutes per day is a good start. There are many methods to choose from. Find one you like that works for you and stick to it to for at least three weeks to see how you feel. There is more information on meditation in Chapter 7.

The only condition required for you to receive clear and honest responses is to have an open mind that's free of trivial personal concerns and preconceived ideas. If you're not getting clear on the responses you're receiving, then you must become clear by bringing to your consciousness any beliefs, self-centered wishes, fears, or doubts operating on an unconscious level. Do this with the *Interview with Your Self* questions and with the help of an honest, modest, and open mind. (See Appendix III for a list of programmed beliefs.)

Gradually you'll cultivate a relationship with your inner source that you won't want to give up. It may happen that if you stop the process, you'll slip back into your old ways. Remember, we do this when we aren't fully conscious. Therefore, if this method doesn't work well for you, try to find one that does, or create your own. It's equally important to set aside the time required for this. It can be done anywhere and anytime, such as seating on a bus or sitting in airports. As a result of weeks, months, and years of sticking to the practice, you'll not only enjoy it, but will become more detached and trusting of the flow of life. You'll experience less stress and fear and life will finally be all you wanted it to be.

Don't worry about becoming disconnected from essence. It may seem to happen at times, but this is because we live in a world that tries to draw us into its materiality through our analytical minds and addictive desires. For example, have you ever been at home happily watching a good movie when, on a commercial break, you get pulled into buying something or are upset about some news? That is the power of the world we live in. Our space is full of information that attaches to us so fast that we don't even notice it. *They* tell you to protect yourself from robbers by buying an alarm; *they* urge you to get the best health insurance or have whiter teeth! Even a casual conversation with a neighbor can result in your being pulled into wanting to go to a party from which you'll arrive home late, thus affecting your ability to handle something important the next day.

Let's revisit the analogy of the chariot. When you become distracted and allow the horses to do as they please, it's similar to doing what you feel is pleasant, desirable, and fun. This is also where your emotions and addictions play a big part. The role of the driver of your intellect is to recall these pieces of information and use them to get clear about what it is that you want the most. The chariot travels best when it goes with the flow and works as a team; the horses, driver, and passenger need to communicate. It might be that you have to tell your horses that they need to wait for something they desire until you complete a project. The responses are always within your reach. We always know, but sometimes we pretend we don't. Be patient and remember to do all things in moderation; don't confuse being patient with overindulging. In the worst-case scenario, we may learn that we didn't make the right decision, but even in those situations, we come away with clarity as to what it is that we don't want or what the next step might be.

We sometimes get confused about what is happening, and before we know it, we start to push against the flow. It's always best to allow the organic process of creation to come into full display.

Being v. Doing

"Life is what happens to you when you are busy making other plans."

—John Lennon, *Beautiful Boy*

Much has been said about how to rid one's self of attachments, how to become detached, and how doing so can lead to a happier life. The problem seems to arise from the notion that not doing somethings is a *useless* approach to life. Nonaction is quite complicated for us. By taking no action, we're, in effect, taking action by default.

By nonaction I mean that which is not carried outwards towards the material world, but is an act carried inside of you. This will be the most important action you have to take to correct yourself, to assist yourself, to allow yourself, and to stop yourself from doing what no longer serves you.

You are always creating your outside actions, but in a completely different way. When at the unconscious level, you didn't take time to consider your actions from the soul perspective. There's a tendency to rush these internal processes and so we fail to evaluate what is really happening. In the same way, we can fail to see all the available responses, not only from the perspective of our minds, but also from our souls. This interview leads us to consider what our inner self is guiding us to do about any given situation. We need to get past our initial survival response. The mind's first response is to see most of our situations in life as a yes or no, now or never, good or bad, or some kind of dualistic notion rooted deeply in fear, pleasure/pain, or in power struggle responses. We need to take action of course, but as an inward movement rather than an external one. Take time, go inside, and answer the questions.

Throughout history we've seen others apply some form of this process. The lives of many saints, scholars, ascended masters, and spiritual teachers, as well as ordinary people who were true to themselves, attest to this fact. It's really so simple when we allow; it doesn't even require moving to a foreign country, joining a particular religion, or associating with any cult. It's merely your personal contribution to make this world a better place. All you need is a commitment "to be your true self."

On a personal note, I consider myself to be a *doer*. I am an action-driven (yang) person. There was a lot to overcome before I could even begin to see the possibilities for myself. I'd experienced so much frustration and doubt. As in the chariot analogy, I'd stopped my horses. These were my inner resistances, the inertia pulling me into old habits and commonly held views that had little to do with my own. A tug of war was going on inside of me, and I was being pulled in many different directions. That's what it feels like when we try to give up our old ways of dealing with life.

For years, I worked as a sales executive. This job required me to travel to many exciting places and put in long, fully scheduled days. In addition to the standard pressures involved in working with international corporations, I also dealt with the competitors, and in my case, I was at times the only female in the room. As much as I enjoyed the work and many of the tasks, the demands of the job pushed me increasingly away from the person I really was. Before I knew it, I ended up wearing a suit attitude even in my free time. It got so bad that I awoke mornings not knowing why I was there. Sometimes I even lost track of where I was at the time. There was too much action, pushing, doing, coming, and going happening at the same time. I didn't know how to stop it, nor did I take the time.

Finally the pain and despair of these activities drove me to look for a solution. I developed my practice to the point that not only was it therapeutic personally, but I felt compelled to help others change their lives. Now in retrospect, I see that it was one of the best decisions I ever made. My practice completely changed the way I experience my day, my work, and the people I came in contact with. When the internal connection is weak, actions are likely to provide disillusionment, anxiety, and conflicts. When harmony prevails on all levels—body, mind, and soul—actions are powerful and creative. When you're being inspired by your soul, life feels softer, lighter, and carefree. No matter what you choose, you'll be searching for answers to life's situations, either from a limiting source or from an infinite source.

Yet we find all sorts of excuses, such as, "I know what is happening," or "I know what others think," or "I know what will happen in the future if I don't do something now!" Ninety-five percent of the time what we play out in our minds won't turn out that way at all. Most of these rationales are not only invalid, but they come from the incorrect perception of the events, people, and oneself. These types of responses are generally based on pre-conceived ideas, beliefs, and notions about yourself, others, and the world. They're logical reasons developed from your analytical mind supporting your programmed beliefs and ideas. (See list of programmed beliefs in Appendix III.)

At first glance, you might think that no questioning in the world would change them. My challenge to you is to put them to the test through a trial period of at least three weeks.

The way of not doing is more an experience than a rule.

Why is that relevant to you now? We're constantly making things better, faster, smarter, or less expensive. We leverage technology or improve processes. In other words, we strive to do more with less. Why should we not apply this *less is better* approach to our lives in general? Is this possible? Ponder the question, "How many times have you had to pay a price for having rushed into what initially seemed the best solution at the time?" Maybe you haven't yet noticed it, but don't be surprised if, when you begin to answer the questions, you find most of the actions that once seemed so logical or necessary are not required at all. In time you'll be happy to see how life opens possibilities you couldn't have even anticipated with careful, extensive planning. You could never have guessed that exact sequence of events, people, situations, or the details that played a part. You'll be amazed at how these led to such a great outcome.

Time is the space for creation to take form; time is a key medium for creation.

Understanding Your Emotions

The energy that feeds our bodies and minds is known in China as chi and in India as prana. Isn't it curious that neither the English nor Spanish languages have an equivalent to these words? We must use a combination of two words in order to convey their meaning; we say life force, life energy, or life intelligence. Therefore, it's quite understandable that we stuck when it comes to differentiating and validating the existence of this force in our lives. When we're connected to the Tao, we feel no resistance at any level; we accept and go with the flow of life. However, the moment we stop being genuine with our thinking, we are no longer true to ourselves. It's at these precise moments that we'll experience negative thought patterns, depression, confusion, and even conflict. They show up as a feeling of lack, dissatisfaction, discontent, or insecurity. If these feelings escalate, they can result in a blockage of the flow of energy and ultimately affect our minds and bodies.

In the ancient medical system of Ayurveda (see Chapter 7), health isn't described as lack of illness or physical symptoms; health for Ayurveda is harmony within our mind, body, and soul. Ayurveda teaches that the root of all illness is an error of the intellect. Although genetic and other factors are also considered, it's an error of the intellect that affects our behaviors and finally results in physical symptoms of illness.

The contradicting ideas or thoughts we hold will always be oppressing our pure spirits. If not dealt with, they will cut the flow of chi or prana, and that will eventually manifest in illness. Hence, the importance of identifying these feelings, emotions, and blockages of our flow of energy as signals or indicators we need to investigate in order to validate our thoughts. The importance of removing these blockages or thoughts is imperative for our well-being; it's best to deal with them as soon as you notice any strange oppression in the chest, nervousness, worry, or even restlessness.

Here are some questions to be considered when trying to identify these patterns of thought:

—Am I scheming or plotting?
—Am I mentally repeating a situation? Can I see the pattern?
—Am I judging others or myself?
—Am I feeling sorry for myself or feeling discouraged?
—Can I not see the end of a situation?
—Am I resisting what is taking place right now?

These questions are all due to a lack of faith in ourselves, others, and/or life. In short, the problems arise when we fail to accept what is happening. This lack of acceptance is because we have little faith in our souls' guidance. That's why the interviewing process of investigating our thoughts (bringing them into our conscious mind) helps us to move forward. Checking the validity of our ideas will move us closer to the root of the problem and provide a new vision.

Problems mostly arise when we stop moving with the flow and put up resistance. We must accept what's happening is for our own benefit. Understand that feelings of resistance will only breed more resistance. It's in our best interest to accept what we don't always see as our highest good. With practice our faith grows because we see in retrospect that the situation was not really as bad as it seemed.

The *I Ching* also shows us that we lose connection with our higher selves when we stop going with the flow (resisting what is happening); when we think of the past (revisiting, wishing, fearing); dwell on the future (imagining, wishing, anticipating); or compare ourselves to others (envy, wishing, judging, expecting). In each of these scenarios we have stopped being in the here and now.

Our thoughts and emotions are so closely related that they seem to be one. In fact, emotions are thoughts that have entered our bodies with their negative or positive energies (peptides). It's well known that our thoughts can weaken us both physically and mentally. Kinesiology studies exactly that. We don't need to be experts in body language to be able to tell what someone else is thinking or what's making that person feel less than whole. If you're close to that person, it's often easy; it can also be just as easy with strangers. They unknowingly communicate without words when they are sad, lost, angry, confused, worried, or in a hurry. Therefore, we only have to become aware of what our emotions are telling us about the thoughts and beliefs we're holding as truth in our minds.

When we're operating predominantly from the analytical side of our mind, we lose connection with the here and now. However, something in that here and now needs your attention and that's your thinking. Your beliefs and ideas about something need to be brought up out of the cave into the light for closer examination. That is the job of your emotions. They act as reinforcement and appreciation of something you like, enjoy, love, or want more of. It's sad when you come to understand this too late. Remember to get clear as you answer the questions in the interview; bring everything into the light.

Emotions can be very powerful at times; they come like waves and they overtake us, so what can we do? Are we doomed to remain prisoners of our emotions? We must cultivate an observer attitude by learning to detach and go inside ourselves before responding or over-reacting. In this way we gain powerful insight into which emotions are driving us. As previously mentioned, emotions are charged with chemicals known as neuropeptides. When released into our bloodstream they act like real drugs feeding the behavior patterns in which we find ourselves trapped.

Emotions are also related to our energy body, prana; they are affected by the blockages that take place in our chakras or energy centers. Ancient sages speak of seven prime energy centers and how closely they're related to our feelings and emotions. In Ayurveda there's a discipline that specializes in the awareness of the energy points in the body; this is also true with Chinese medicine. The main energy points in acupuncture and the chakras in Ayurveda are also known and used in the exercises in yoga, martial arts, and other ancient disciplines.

The book, *Interview with Your Body* expands on the point that the survival patterns we've been hard-wired for in our chakras also have a big impact on our day-to-day responses to events and situations. These have to do with the three lower chakras' conditioned responses to our needs. Our main needs are for safety when in danger, nourishment of the body, and the power to feel in control of our lives. The body, in fact, does not respond to what happens, but rather to our *belief* about what is happening. If we perceive a situation as a threat, our bodies will react with a fight-or-flight response. Regardless of what the real situation is, our bodies will release into our blood stream all the chemicals required to perform the task. This happens because we hold limited and distorted visions of our world and what is actually occurring. In these instances, we are reacting rather than responding. It's our instinct to react out of wanting to protect our basic survival needs, but these reactions are usually based on imaginary threats or fears. Despite the fact that many of us have everything we need to survive on a daily basis, we still react in this way. This is because we are always looking to the future, remembering the past, comparing ourselves with others, or failing to see that, for now, everything is fine.

Imagine that you are at home happily watching a movie when a commercial for a home security system comes up on your TV screen. If you don't have an alarm already installed, you could very easily engage in this particular commercial. You were feeling fine and relaxed just before it came on. At that moment you might even recall a conversation at the neighborhood grocery store about the old couple in #15 whose home was broken into last week. Now, out of the blue, you feel a need to protect yourself and your house, despite the fact that everything else is just as it was before the commercial. The truth is that nothing has made you perceive any danger—nothing but your ideas. You're now more likely to buy that advertised alarm. These sales ploys are very powerful and successful, luring us to participate even unconsciously. They engage us from the perception about something we need to do in order to be safe. But we can never be 100 percent safe. Therefore, it is an illusion that we are buying into. Although when you look at the grander scheme of things, the deeper truth is that you're never in danger, even if your physical body dies, because all that changes is our form.

New information provided by scientific studies on the addictive nature of emotions can be used to our advantage. We know which of our emotions are creating the most suffering in our lives. If in doubt, go within to ask your inner self. Then make a decision to give up your anger, your sadness, your need to control your fears, or your worry. Identify the emotion as it comes over you; watch your physical response to it and accept it without resistance.

This process enables us to rid our lives of painful experiences. Letting go of a painful emotion rids us of our addictive, programmed responses (peptides) in the body, much like giving up alcohol, cigarettes, or any other drug.

Keep notes on your progress, reward yourself, and be patient and understanding with yourself. If you've given in or failed to fully let go of a particular emotion, you can still make the choice to change your mind about how you respond the next time. (See the Table of Emotions in Appendix I and Appendix II.)

For example, if I've failed to eliminate anger in a situation, I then change the need to revisit the situation with anger. Perhaps I'm somewhere with a friend and get carried away talking about politics. I even fully engage in frustrating feelings and emotions. Before I realize it, I become very angry. When I become conscious of what just transpired, I have the opportunity to make another choice. I can then choose to give it up or not.

It is also an opportunity to better understand that everyone can make a mistake in terms of being confused and acting out of distorted ideas about how things are.

Our goal is to be emotionally detached from situations we are involved in. As the emotions arise, we observe them and try to feel them fully in our bodies. We can also close our eyes, observe them, and then make a conscious decision to change them. Observing emotions tends to disperse them.

Exercise: With eyes closed, stop to observe where in the body you feel the emotion; consciously breathe into the emotion and go deeply into it. Then release it by breathing out the emotion. Pause and observe again; has it changed? Repeat the exercise until you feel the emotion disappear.

This is a powerful exercise that I've used with clients even during emergency calls. They soon were able to get out of the emotional wave that trapped them. The intensity then decreased to the point at which they were able to change their focus to something more productive.

By doing this we are able to give up what's making us become emotionally involved. Whether it is an argument or a resistance to something or someone, we give it up. This surrender dissipates the anger and we are then able to move on to something else. We also need to give up expectations of how things should go or be if that is what is creating the emotions and keeping us from going with the flow. It's also important that, at highly charged emotional moments, we remember the process of association our minds use when thinking. In this way we deliberately stop it; otherwise, the process continues to fill our mental space with more thoughts and keeps fueling our emotional state creating a vortex of negativity. A vortex such as this will fill up your mental space and engage your mind and body in addictive behaviors.

This is the reason why observing the emotions in the body is so powerful. When faced with long periods of tension and emotional turmoil, it's better to take it one day at a time. There will be moments when it may be important to do nothing: no interview, no thinking, no revisiting. Just completely switch off. Later, when you are feeling recovered, you can go inside, examine what is happening, and interview your self with love, honesty and patience.

Because

"It is because you are in the dark,
that you search for light.

It is because you have been happy,
that you know when you are sad.

It is because you missed the path,
that you found a way.

It is because of you that the stars light up,
and the whole drama of life takes
the universe's stage once again."

Please don't feel that all this is a huge endeavor; lighten up, see it as an adventure; you are always creating your life anew. Nothing is yet defined; we need now, more than ever, to become clear. As individual observers, we create and collectively cocreate our realities. Thus, we are all creating these changes right down to the details. It's inevitable that somehow we'll evolve into a more connected worldwide community, despite all of our differences. We all have the same basic concerns, wishes, and tribulations. Don't we all have a natural instinct to work together to create more of the solutions that are positive for the whole? It's ironic that at this moment in history, there are so many without jobs. There's so much work to be done; here are some examples:

—Get new transportation systems for our roads.
—Get new cars that respect our environment.
—Clean the water that sustains us.
—Create healthier sustainable farming and agriculture.
—Get new financial systems in place.
—Educate our children about new truths and concepts.
—Have new energy generating systems that are greener and accessible to all.
—Have a new medical vision that treats us at all levels; body, mind, and soul.

—Put into place new governments that sustain and respect us all as one big family, sharing a great, loving, and living planet.

These are just a few of the things waiting to be done. Isn't it encouraging to imagine what we can accomplish if we collectively commit to taking the first steps?

Chapter 6

THE INTERVIEW WITH YOUR SELF

This chapter will describe the interview process and offer effective ways to use it. It's a tool you can use often. Just as with clients who come to me with worries, anxiety, and despair, my goal is to help you think more clearly so you can then discern your own answers. This is the starting point in the process of getting your life back on track and free of external influences that are taking you where you don't wish to go. There are three main layers to our existence. Within these three layers we can distinguish another three (see Layers of Life in the next chapter). Be as honest with yourself as possible in responding to the interview questions. It is a powerful tool revealing to us the exact information we need at any given moment. It's a simple process that you can do anywhere; all you need are the questions, a little time and space to be alone, and the will to listen to the answers you are given.

When I started the journaling process at home, I created a sacred space for myself. Please don't rush the interview process; make this an experience. Create a nice space in a quiet room at home—somewhere you like to sit comfortably. Light a scented candle or scent stick if you have one. Keep your pen and paper handy or a journaling book/pad. It's nice to be able to go back and re-read them later to see how much has changed. On the other hand, the areas in which you've remained stuck will become more pronounced.

Sections of the interview are also divided into three parts: body, mind, and soul.

Body—For the purpose of the interview, this part relates to your physical self and all that is part of your physical existence: your body, your property, your finances, and your physical environment.

Mind—This relates to your thoughts, ideas, beliefs, intellect, and the process of logic, as well as your memory data bank.

Soul—This is your spirituality, your network of helpers, your practice, your connection to your higher self, and to the Tao or whatever belief system you relate to. It also includes your personal gifts and uniqueness.

To answer the questions, please refer to the instructions and apply them to your specific details, as they're currently present in your life situation.

In the beginning you'll feel drawn to query yourself about situations that aren't moving in the direction you want. These might be areas you're emotionally involved in or distressed by, like the end of a relationship, the promotion you wanted and failed to get, or any situation that's not turning out how you had hoped. Describe the situation briefly (in a sentence or two) at the top of each page of Section One and Two.

If nothing's distressing you at that moment, then just consider a particular situation you are either curious or uncertain about. Practice doing the sections daily; it's best to take a week to read each section of the book. For example, take the bellow Section One questions and then read that section of the book for the day before moving on to Section Two. (see chapter 5)

Before you begin, please see the examples of an interview in Appendix IV.

Section One

SITUATION: _____ (Write out the situation here that you are addressing before answering the questions).

BODY—With regards to this situation, consider the following:

1) What part of my body am I most often aware of? Why do I think my focus is there?
   Response:

Contd. -Section One Body

2) What part of my body may I be neglecting because of this? Why is that?
   Response:

3) What emotions are engaging me in an emotional reaction with regards to this?
   Response:

4) Where in my body do I feel a disconnection when thinking about this situation? (Close your eyes and search for the sensations arising in your body.)
   Response:

5) What physical activities am I experiencing issues with because of this situation? Consider sleep, eating issues, pain issues, exercising, working, relaxing, relating with others, or anything else that may be pertinent.
   Response:

6) Who or what has been triggering my emotional responses as a result of this situation?
   Response:

7) What do I spend most of my day doing with regards to the situation? (Reflect here on money, time, energy, efforts, sabotage, etc.)
   Response:

8) What activities make me feel physically exhausted?
   Response:

9) How do I think my environmental surroundings are affecting this situation?
   Response:

SITUATION: _____

MIND—With regard to this situation I am concerned about:

1) What thoughts are occupying most of my mental space at this time? List a minimum of three, and a maximum of six.
Response:

2) Can I see any connections between the above thoughts?
Response:

3) Can I identify any of them as playing a significant role in the situation? Am I able to choose one as the most influential?
Response:

4) What's my first thought in the morning and my last thought at night?
Response:

5) What thought is affecting my relationship with other(s)? (Example: scarcity, jealousy, envy, angry thoughts, sadness, etc.)
Response:

6) How is this thought affecting my relationship with other(s)?
Response:

7) What are the excuses, logic, or planning running through my mental screen? Could any of these be creating the situation?
Response:

8) How does this situation match my story (past experience, projecting future, observing the world, etc.)
Response:

9) What ideas are contributing to my feeling bad, weak, or overloaded? (Note any mental images.)
Response:

SITUATION: _____

SOUL—When responding to the questions, try to give the most honest response that comes as a gut feeling.

1) Do the ideas I hold about this situation come from any of the dualistic limitations, such as love/hate, good/bad, pleasure/pain, justice/injustice, etc.
   Response:

2) Are these ideas true and relevant to me? Could they be coming from the influence of society, friends, information picked up from studies, TV, or religious beliefs?
   Response:

3) Are these ideas pushing me towards destructive actions, thoughts, and emotions toward myself and/or others?
   Response:

4) When I feel bad or am in panic mode, how do I expect this situation to turn out? What does my intuition say v. my internal chatter?
   Response:

5) Are my ideas, plans, and actions a quick fix rather than a fearless, ego-less, response? Do these ideas, plans, and actions allow for spontaneity, synchronicity, or changes?
   Response:

6) How are these ideas affecting me now on an inner level? Does they feel right? Do they hold traces of life beliefs on karma, suffering, or learning struggles?
   Response:

7) How do they separate me from the here and now? Do they enable me to get on with what's in front of me? (Wondering about tomorrow, yesterday, and what if?)
   Response:

Contd. -Section One Soul

8) How do I imagine myself responding—acting or not—on this situation? Can I feel any resistance?
Response:

9) Am I emotionally detached from the final outcome or result?
Response:

For the second part of the interview process, please take some breathing space before moving into it in order to allow your soul to inspire you.

Section Two

When you respond to the following questions, imagine that you have this situation already solved in a desirable manner. What would that look like? Then respond to the question honestly.

Remember: Body is the part that relates to your physical circumstances. Mind relates to your thoughts, ideas, and logic. The soul relates to your higher self, your spirituality, and your purposes in life.

BODY—If this situation were already resolved to your satisfaction, what would that look like?

SITUATION: _____

1) How does this situation feel in my body and how does it affect my energy levels?
Response:

2) What changes in physical activities would I make so that my body feels well?
Response:

Contd. -Section Two Body

3) When visualizing this outcome, what part of my body do I feel
   most connected to?
   Response:

4) What physical activities do I enjoy the most?
   Response:

5) Where in this world do I see myself living or spending most of
   my time?
   Response:

6) Who would contribute most to my feelings of being relaxed and
   loved? (It could be more than one person or pet(s).)
   Response:

7) How would I spend my time in activities related to work and
   leisure?
   Response:

8) How do I see myself spending my money? On what type of goods,
   energy, or quality of time?
   Response:

9) Where in my body do I feel gratitude, peace, and joy?
   Response:

MIND—If this situation were already resolved in the manner you want,
what would that look like?

SITUATION: _____

1) What thoughts would occupy most of my mental space? List a
   minimum of three and a maximum of six.
   Response:

Contd. -Section Two Mind

2) What emotions would these thoughts trigger in me?
   Response:

3) What do I think would be my first and last thought each day?
   Response:

4) How do I think these thoughts would affect my relationships?
   Response:

5) How is my logical rationale working best in order to create more of these experiences? (Consider trust, service, love, compassion, giving, etc.)
   Response:

6) How does this situation fit in with my personal life experience? (Give three examples.)
   Response:

7) What ideas or images feel the most empowering in this experience?
   Response:

8) How do I help others to experience similar situations?
   Response:

9) How do others help me in this situation?
   Response:

SOUL—If this situation were already resolved in the manner of your choosing, what would that look like? Consider yourself to be limitless when responding.

SITUATION: _____

1) How would this situation make me feel in the long term, and will it still be relevant?
   Response:

Contd. -Section Two Soul

2) Now that things have turned around, what do I value most from this experience?
    Response:

3) What do I wish to do for others from where I stand now?
    Response:

4) What would I like to do most? What would be second and third choices?
    Response:

5) What are my unique gifts and talents?
    Response:

6) Where in my daily activities and interactions can I express them?
    Response:

7) What spiritual practices will I incorporate?
    Response:

8) What will be my personal slogans or mantras?
    Response:

9) Write a sentence that defines how I see myself and what my gifts are.
    Response:

10) Are the above answers offering a fulfilling and engaging perspective of my life? I In what way?
    Response:

Conclusions

Once you finish answering all the questions, please compare your responses in Part One with responses in Part Two.

—Do they differ much?
—Do you see a recurring pattern?
—What steps can you take to keep the feelings authentic?
—How can you continue to experience these feelings for longer periods of time?

The goal of these exercises is to assist you to become clear on what the dynamics are between your body, mind, and soul. They are designed to help you use all of these parts to create a state of being that is closer to what you prefer. These exercises will also allow you to make any necessary changes to your ideas and concepts about situations and external circumstances. Your thoughts and ideas always play an important role in your routine reactions or responses.

With consistency and time you'll get closer to what you really desire. In some cases you will actually eliminate a large amount of suffering connected with the imbalance and inconsistency between your body, mind, and soul. This result will open the door to peace and love. Remember, the *master* is the one whose responses to the first part of the interview most closely match the responses of the second part of the interview.

You may've heard the expression, "In the world, but not of it." There's no pressure for you to pursue mastery. It's only important that you gain a clear understanding of where a life free from pain and worry over earthly concerns lies. Remember also that these concerns will keep arising because they are hardwired in us; this is an organic process and will take some time to accomplish.

If you are short of time and unable to do the complete section, at least do Section One. It will allow you to see where you are getting stuck; when you have the time, do the interview again completely.

Some of us have difficulty in the beginning identifying what it is that we really want. If that is your case, you can periodically explore some difficult areas by answering the following questions:

1) When have I been most satisfied in my life?
2) What situations, ideas, and beliefs got in the way?
3) How do these sometimes overshadow my happiness?
4) What is my superpower, my spirit animal, or God/Goddess?
5) What do others say that I do well?
6) What do others say that I am not so good at?
7) What things do I enjoy doing so much that I lose track of time?
8) What things do I not like doing at all?
9) Imagine yourself a year from now celebrating what a great year it has been for you. What would that look like? List this in terms of body, mind, and soul.

When asking others for their input, be sure to ask those who can give you an honest response. Don't allow the mind/ego to become too involved.

Express Version of the Interview

Whenever you feel the need throughout your day to get back to yourself, use this version.

Consider the situation that's affecting you that you wish to explore quickly. Then fill in the blanks in the nine sentences below. Example: I now choose to feel peace v. feeling anxious and nervous; I now choose to trust my friends' ability to solve their own problems v. telling them what to do. Basically it's to assist you in experiencing what you want v. what you're experiencing at the moment. Once again, remember that body makes reference to your physical being and welfare and mind to your ideas, emotions, and beliefs. Lastly, your soul refers to your inner desires, feelings, and wishes. (See Appendix V for examples.)

Body (Insert your situation.)

1) **I now feel _____ v. what I was feeling _____.**

2) **I have _____ v. having or not having now _____.**

3) **I do _____ v. having to do _____.**

67

Mind (Insert your situation.)

1) I choose to think _____ v. thinking that _____.

2) I now choose _____ v. having to _____.

3) I choose to do _____ v. doing _____.

Soul (Insert your situation.)

1) I am being _____ v. I want to be _____.

2) I am grateful for _____ v. I wish _____.

3) I see possibilities _____ v. limitations _____.

You can adjust the beginnings and the words provided above as needed, but it's important to do the three layers of body, mind, and soul to the best of your ability. The goal of using *versus* is to help you compare both options. In doing so you'll gain clarity about the space you're now occupying at the levels of the body, mind, and soul v. the spaces that you could choose to occupy.

We gain clarity over our confusing ideas, thoughts, and beliefs by bringing them to our conscious attention. It is then easier to reframe those thoughts to allow harmony with what are our true wishes and essence.

In the example presented, the participant taking the express version is feeling fed- up with her work and financial situation. However, the fears and beliefs keeping her in that situation need further investigation, such as what's frightening and why is it frightening? What will it take to remove that fear? Once we gain clarity, then we move into a more powerful position; we stop looking for the blockages and we start looking for options and new ideas to take us away from those limiting beliefs. We come to realize that we're frightened because we've only considered one possible outcome instead of all the possibilities. We are focusing on the negative alone causing a strong feeling of fear. The truth is that we don't know for certain what will be the outcome; anything is possible in the long or short term.

We need to clean our internal environment daily so that we don't continuously ruminate about the same ideas and beliefs that keep creating unwanted emotions and feelings. Once we empty our internal space, creativity can take place away from our deeply rooted, hard-wired reactions. Our personal ideas and beliefs are deeply rooted in our society's belief systems. We have incorporated these into our egos and adopted them as our personality attributes. Some of these structures and models need to be dismantled so that we may connect with who we really are. With time and patience we come to see that the ideas that hold us back are not really a part of our natural being and that we can discredit them and let them go.

This is the reason why adversity enters our lives—to make us question these beliefs and ideas. When things are running smoothly we are not likely to question the structures and the models; we're too busy enjoying ourselves. To put it a little differently, it's through adversity that we bypass limiting structures and move into a new way of being that's in line with who we are now.

Doubt the Door into the Fear Room

When in doubt, it's best to wait until we get out of our emotional perceptions and then proceed after we've cleared our minds with the interview process.

When we doubt others, we've become attached to some belief of how they should be or shouldn't be. This does not provide a spiritual space and time for their own development. It will be helpful if we recall how many times we've failed to do or be who we really are. Understanding that everyone goes through life with a certain amount of programmed beliefs always helps us to be patient. It is necessary to keep relationships real; we cannot expect from others anything we ourselves find difficult to do. This realization can help us to develop detachment and respect for others' beliefs, decisions, and choices.

In addition, the *I Ching* warns against going in the opposite direction. We must be careful not to feel superior or think we have all the answers. If we get too proud and push others, we should consider it a signal showing us that we've moved to the other end of the spectrum. We are then operating out of our egos' distorted perception of our uniqueness, believing we're so special that we're superior. It's important to clear your mind of these thoughts; otherwise, you'll start to cling to that projected image of yourself. We must recall that attachment will always result in pain, and that modesty and love are the best allies to have under any circumstance.

When we doubt the Tao, we are obstructing the flow of chi or prana— the greater intelligence operating behind the scenes. We move away from accepting the way things are and the power that lies with this acceptance. This power is directly related to our trust in the way things are. When we trust we are free of thoughts of negativity, separation, and attachment to a certain outcome. Recall the many times in our lives that we've felt doubt and how things have always worked out for the best after all. Sometimes this means we must first come to terms with it and accept the fact that things we consider unacceptable when we first encountered them, really are not.

In order to restore our connection with the Tao we need to stop doing, thinking, or resisting whatever is blocking this connection and keeping us separated. From experience I find that I need to get busy (occupied v. preoccupied); if I am with others, I can decide to deliberately choose to refrain from speaking or change the subject if possible. We all know when we've become detached or when we're back in balance. The first sign is that our bodies, minds, and souls feel released.

Why am I so certain this is going to work? First, because of my personal experience; but you need to experience this for yourself. When in the midst of doubt, do the following exercise:

—Recall a project or accomplishment that you consider to be the most significant in your life, career, or another area.
—Why do you think it happened?
—How do you think you created it?
—Did you ever envision something like that taking place before the event?
—Journal how a specific accomplishment you achieved in the past is a good indicator that proves that you will thrive in this new situation.

Stories and analogies act as powerful reminders that stick to us visually and contextually. Let me tell you a story that Osho (an Indian spiritual leader) told to his Sannyasins (disciples). It's a story about the fortunes and misfortunes of a villager. It's about a man who had a very nice horse that was so rare everyone wanted to buy it from him at any price. Then one day his horse was gone.

The entire village gathered to sympathize and they said, "How unfortunate! You could have sold it, but you were too stubborn and now it is gone."

The old man laughed and responded, "Don't talk nonsense! Only say that the horse is no longer in the stable."

Fifteen days later the horse came back, but not alone; it brought a dozen wild horses with it from the forest.

The whole village gathered and they said, "The old man was right! His horse is back and has brought twelve beautiful horses with it. Now he can earn as much money as he wants." They said apologetically to him, "We cannot know the ways of God, but that was great! You knew or saw a glimpse into the future."

He told them, "I cannot predict the future; all I know is that the horse has come back with twelve other horses. What is going to happen tomorrow, no one knows."

The very next day, it happened that the old man's only son was trying to break in one of the new horses and fell and broke his legs. Everyone in town again gathered and said, "One never knows; you were right, it has proved to be a curse. It would have been better if the horse had never come back. Your son will remain crippled for the rest of his life."

The old man said, "Just wait and see what happens. All we can say is that my son has broken his legs; that's all."

Within two weeks all of the young men in the village were called away by the government because their country was at war. Only the old man's son was left because he was useless to fight.

The townspeople gathered and said, "Our sons are gone! At least you have your son. He is crippled, but he is here! Our sons are all going to be killed."

Again the old man would only reply, "I'll say only this much. Your sons have been taken by the government. My son has been left, but there is no conclusion."

What I conclude from Osho's story is that worry is useless. The mechanics of the mind displayed in this story keep the villagers under threat—always anticipating, always somewhere else, resisting what is. They were suffering as if they were riding an emotional carrousel, while the old man always stayed in tune and balanced. (You can find this story and many other stories in *Osho's Tarot Deck*.)

I invite you from now on to view emotions as signals that we've been drawn into a particular story. Emotions can help us to regain consciousness and to put us back in a more powerful state of being. Hence, we can also say that our emotions act at times like blessings in disguise.

Chapter 7

HEALING THE BODY, MIND, AND SPIRIT

New and Old Paradigms Coming Together

A new paradigm is emerging in medicine that integrates the physical and nonphysical body. This paradigm doesn't consider the human body as a separate entity without a relationship to the nonphysical components of life. We now know, for example, that we're constantly interchanging with our environment. Viruses that move from one person to another use this nonphysical connection. We know that our well-being also extends to the space around us. This space has changed the perception of our bodies, and it's no longer limited to physical body dimensions.

Scientists now understand that our physical world is made up of consciousness. In recent years, studies have shown how our own individual consciousness affects the space of the collective consciousness. Thousands of years ago the *Vedanta* tradition of India presented a model of life that explained the connection to our environment using seven *Koshas*, or layers that I will briefly refer to. Ady Shankara, who lived in the eighth century, also identified and studied these three layers in the following table:

Table I—Table of Koshas and Systems Treating Them

ANNAMAYA KOSHA	PRANAMAYA KOSHA	MANNOMAYA KOSHA
PHYSIOLOGICAL BODY	LIFE FORCE CHI-PRANA	MIND AND INTELLECT
GENETIC AND PHYSICAL TRAITS	HOLDS TOGETHER BOTH PHYSICAL AND NONPHYSICAL	EGO
MEDICAL TREATMENTS	ACUPUNCTURE, YOGA	MIND THERAPY

The three major layers of the body are categorized above to demonstrate the need to balance these layers, along with some techniques to implement them. However, the above graph isn't displaying the soul completely. In the Vedanta tradition seven layers cover the soul. For now, we'll slowly introduce these dimensions of your- self through the interview process, and in the books to come, *Interview With Your Body* and *Interview With Your Soul.* To achieve harmony at all levels, we need to create and experience life at all levels. We're living simultaneously at all of these levels and are really spiritual beings having a physical experience. We are not our bodies, not our minds, nor are we only our souls. We are spaceless, timeless beings and we will never die. The later will be expanded in more detail in *Interview with Your Soul.*

From ancient tradition and through the work of many physicists who are studying at a quantum level, we know there is much more going on in nonspace than meets the eye. We are all made up of the nonphysical; our physical body is also part of the physicality we see around us. This coincides, too, with the new paradigm emerging in modern medicine that I'll refer to here as *integrative medicine.* According to Ayurveda (the medicinal system that originated in India over 3000 years ago), the human body is like a river of information or intelligence that creates our physical experiences and our bodies.

"I am that, you are that, and 'that' is all there is."

—Vedic saying.

I began to use the principles of Ayurveda to get my body in balance and have been teaching others to do so now for some years. I've found these tools to be powerful in creating balance at all levels of life. In fact, just by simply doing a test of our *doshas* (mind and body patterns) and a quick check-up of the person, it's quite easy to predict a large percentage of his or her behaviors. This has been a positive step in speeding up the therapeutic process.

Ayurveda can be used as a preventive tool, as well as a corrective one, and can be used in conjunction with traditional western medicine. From my own experience and with clients, I can conclude that if you live according to the Ayurvedic principles, you'll find it easy to integrate mind, body, and soul. It's central to assisting anyone who wants to maintain balance at these three levels. There are nine beneficial activities that Ayurveda recommends to keep in balance.

According to Ayurveda, our bodies are the end product of our experiences or the sum of them all. We metabolize our experiences. Haven't you noticed that some people who have very pleasant experiences look young, healthy, peaceful, and happy? On the other hand, you've surely noticed the opposite with people who've had many struggles and problems in their life; they can't hide it in their faces. Their body shows what toll the experiences of the past have had on their body. The lesson is to pay attention to what your body's telling you now in order to know what it will be like in the future.

Proper nourishment is very important to keep the body, mind, and soul in balance and working efficiently. In Ayurveda this involves taking the best from our environment and nourishing ourselves; it involves nutrition, exercise, relaxation, detoxification, and rejuvenation. Here are some quick tips to get you started.

Healing the Body through the Doshas

These are the basic mind and body patterns of Ayurveda prototypes that influence us. They provide nutrition advice and promote healing practices for the body and the mind. There are three doshas or basic body and mind metabolic forces: Vata, Pitta, and Kapha. Each of us is influenced by the doshas, but only one or two are predominant and that's what is known as your dosha.

I invite you to take the test yourself and find out about your mind and body interaction at the level of the doshas. You'll be as surprised as I was. Go to www.innerwise-self.com. Take the doshas test, and I'll send you a brief general profile free of charge.

The doshas affect us at physiological levels as well. For example, they influence our food preferences, body temperature, sleep patterns, weight gain, digestion, and all of our physiological activity and characteristics. With which of the doshas do you most identify? Here is how each of them responds to stress:

Vata: It's my fault (internal mind turmoil).
Pitta: What's wrong with them (blaming others).
Kapha: I don't know (hide from the situation).

The interview process is a powerful tool to help with mind patterns.

1) Ayurvedic Diet

Nutrition in Ayurveda involves using the energy and information in our environment and metabolizing it into our mind and bodies. Hence, we are what we eat; the quality, quantity, and properties of what we eat are of great importance when nourishing our bodies at these micro levels. In Sanskrit, the body is called *Annamayakosha*. It literarily means *the body made of food*.

Interview with Your Body will introduce you to the recommended diet and related concepts. It will also introduce you to a detoxification program you can carry out at home.

If we consider the above premise that we are what we eat, we have to stop contaminating our food chain and Mother Earth; otherwise, we won't be able to continue to create good quality, healthy bodies.

2) Exercise according to Your Dosha.

The light balance and coordination movements are more in balance with Vata, while cardiovascular exercises are good for both Pitta and Kapha. According to this, it's recommended that you match your dosha with your exercise intensity and routine. With Vata, it's better to do low-stamina exercises, such as bicycle riding, yoga, dance, or Pilates. With Pitta, you'll benefit from swimming and will also enjoy a less competitive sport like tennis. With Kapha, the emphasis should be on endurance, with exercise such as jogging, weight training, or vigorous bicycling.

There is also a warning here. Ayurveda recommends that we don't overdo exercise. It needs to be combined with correct breathing (deeply and through the nose). For maximum effectiveness, it's best to utilize a variety of exercises.

Yoga is the Sanskrit word for union and refers to the union of body movement, breathing, and the life force. It also means union with our higher source.

I've created a step-by-step online program to implement these principles at www.innerwise-self.com. The program covers exercises appropriate for any doshas and age that positively influence the emotions, as well as affect our bodies' addictive behaviors.

Once you're in a tailored exercise routine (as described in the book, *Interview with Your Body*), do your best to stick to it for a minimum of three weeks.

3) Healing the Mind through Doshas

By taking care to balance your doshas through your daily activities, diet, and exercise, you're also eliminating distractions that create problems at the mind level. For example, I've noticed that most clients suffering from insomnia are Vata. It's less common in Kapha because the metabolism of Vata, when under stress, will have a tendency to suffer from insomnia. On the other hand, in Ayurveda Kapha individuals tend to stay up late into the night, which creates problems for them. This usually makes them slow starters in the morning. It's the same with Pitta's strong will, providing them endurance and drive. However, when out of balance, it can push them into a life of workaholic patterns and highly competitive behaviors.

4) Healing the Soul through the Doshas

In order to connect with your soul, it's necessary to be conscious of what you're being, instead of what you're doing. This *being* is the pure experience that's free of judgments. For example, you can be at peace by resting in silence, by taking a walk in nature, or you can be humorous by making jokes. This implies that there's a doer and an experiencer; your soul is always the experiencer (not your thinking mind.) Your thinking mind is always attached to the boundaries of roles and bodily function.

Be whatever it is that you want to be (from your soul's perspective, not from mind or fear). Getting clear about what feels good to you and making a conscious decision to move into that space, is the path to the soul. You could use all or any of the following tools for support.

5) Music Therapy

There's a growing body of strong evidence on the results of the wonderful, powerful benefits of music therapy. The use of music in the human evolutionary process can be traced to the early stages of evolution. Music has been accompanying most of the social events of humans throughout history.

Music therapy is now highly evolved and widely used in many different fields. It's a popular therapy in healing (with babies and children), and in psychiatry (with adults and children). Other areas in which it is effective are special education, brain injury, geriatrics, and even in preventive medicine. The reason why it's so powerful therapeutically is because it affects humans at many levels: biological, psychological, intellectual, social, and spiritual. It's quite a comprehensive tool that shouldn't be underestimated. Although music therapy is a specialty that requires qualification, we can all make good use of the music that surrounds us to heal ourselves. Music is one of the most powerful tools to soothe the soul and create a given mood. It can transport people to a pleasant space mentally and physically, stimulate their creativity, and release stress.

There is also vibration therapy, which can be done with different instruments, such as a flute or quartz bowls. These are also techniques used by the Tibetan healing systems; if you have the opportunity to acquire a singing bowl and/or a quartz bowl, use it for your meditation and bodywork. They are also highly enjoyable and therapeutic when used as accompaniment to singing mantras. Vibration therapy is a powerful tool that can assist your healing process at a level that only few methods can do. It's a fast way of changing your mood.

6) Aroma Therapy

This is another very powerful tool; you can use candles, essential oils in your bath, sense sticks, and *rupas* (perfumed body roll bars).

Ayurveda recommends that we do a self-massage once a day, preferably in the morning. You only need a few minutes for it to work. All treatments in Ayurveda have a massage technique that's also adapted for each dosha. A deep, relaxing massage would be ideal for Vata, a cooling and relaxing massage for Pitta, and an invigorating massage would be recommended for Kapha. You will notice the difference within the first few days. Body massage by a therapist can also be done when needed. Our skin is the largest organ in the body; by massaging, you access many nerve endings.

Choose oils according to your dosha (see *www.innerwise-self.com*). Vata Base oils: almond and sesame. Aromatic oils: ylang-ylang, orange, geranium. Pitta Base oils: onagre and evening primrose. Aromatic: sandalwood, jasmine, mint. Kapha Base oils: linseed and sesame. Aromatic: lavender, clove, camphor.

7) Meditation

Meditation should also be considered as part of our routine hygiene. Why? Because it's the best way to keep our mental space clean. We could say that meditation is the practice that allows us to access the silent spaces in our minds. It's important for us to establish this connection in order to create and enhance a transformation vortex to allow the experience our soul.

Mantras are instruments of the mind. They also help you create a vibrational vortex that enhances your meditation process; mantras are primordial sounds and sacred words. They are, in a way, a form of prayer for those who prefer it. Praying is powerful when it builds trust and union to your essence.

The benefits of practicing meditation are numerous. At the physiological level, some benefits are balancing high blood pressure, decreasing muscle tension, and enhancing the immune system. Some of the psychological benefits are an increase in emotional stability, creativity, and self-esteem. Meditation is also a practice that enhances spirituality in many ways, such as increasing compassion and enlarging one's perspective and wisdom. We can say that the practice of meditation is a very important tool for attaining and maintaining body, mind, and soul balance. In meditation, you can also use questions such as, "Who am I? What do I want? How can I help?" This method is known as self-enquiry.

Link to and access a free-guided meditation at www.innerwise-self.com.

8) Communion with Nature

Find a way to spend time with nature and animals. Being indoors for extended periods of time can make us feel restricted at the levels of mind, body, and soul. Hence get out and commune with nature as often as you can.

Regaining balance is an organic process that requires time. Introduce changes gradually and make it a point to try them for at least three weeks before dismissing them. Get busy creating the life you want to live now; don't delay it, because it could possibly be the most important decision you'll ever make. Your life is a road full of enigmas; with the right tools, it can be exciting and enjoyable most of the time—despite what life brings to you. If you can be in harmony, you stand a good chance of staying in balance through changes. Please give yourself only the best; do not neglect any of your vital needs. You are the only one who can make sure these needs are met, and that you always stay true to yourself at every level.

9) Having a Spiritual Network

A spiritual network of people with whom you can share your ideas and situations (without judgment) is a beneficial component of growth and balance. It's important to have an outlet for discussion of your beliefs and spiritual life with like-minded souls. For further information on this topic, see www.innerwise-self.com (English) or www.cosmos-zen.com (Spanish).

Conclusion

The days when spiritual practices were carried out in faraway Eastern countries on a remote mountain, in a monastery, or in an ashram embracing a specific discipline or a dogma are long gone. Creating our spiritual practice need not be an arduous or difficult task. It merely requires consistency and discipline. The idea that spirituality is for a particular type of person, or an ordained or qualified person, is misleading and keeps you out of balance and out of touch with your wise inner self. Many of us have made the mistake of removing ourselves from the equation without knowing that we were imposing limitations on our quality of life. The spiritual dimension of humanity should be seen like any other natural activity, such as eating or exercising. Life becomes balanced when we cultivate a spiritual practice because it is a natural part of our makeup. It's by not doing so that we fail to acknowledge those aspects of ourselves (our bodies, minds, and souls) that need to interact and work together.

Thankfully, the spiritual knowledge and secrets of the ancient sages and enlightened beings of the past are within our reach, as well as the wisdom of those who are here with us now. Many have dedicated their lives to the work of translating, disseminating information to Western cultures, and enlarging this body of knowledge and practices. They do so in a way that benefits many through sharing the essence of the Holy Scriptures and ancient systems of thought.

It's now within our power to study them, to research them, and to find out how we can adapt them to our lives. Many opportunities exist to develop our spiritual lives to whatever level we desire. We are all spiritual beings, and as such, we are never far from the opportunity to find our way back home to our hearts.

All the best,
Mercedes Tur Escriva

APPENDICES

Appendix I

TABLE OF EMOTIONS

EMOTION	RELATED EMOTIONS
LOVE	Affection, empathy, trust, devotion, tenderness, kindness, acceptance, gentleness, affinity, gratitude, veneration, warmth, sympathy, adoration
HAPPINESS	Excitement, fun, pleasure, euphoria, gratification, ecstasy, relief, thrill, contentment, enthusiasm
FEAR	Panic, shock, anxiety, apprehension, uncertainty
ANGER	Fury, resentment, tension, animosity, irritability, hostility, violence, jealousy, envy, hate
SHAME	Guilt, shyness, insecurity, embarrassment, modesty, humiliation, regret
SURPRISE	Confusion, bewilderment, shock, amazement
JOY	Peace, tranquility, bliss, satisfaction, well-being, delight
AVERSION	Hostility, animosity, resentment, rejection, disgust
SADNESS	Disappointment, grief, depression, frustration, loneliness, self-pity, sorrow, despair, pessimism, melancholy, pain, apathy, homesickness

Appendix II

TABLE OF EMOTIONS CLASSIFIED BY BODY, MIND AND SOUL

EMOTION	RELATED EMOTIONS
LOVE	Soul natural responses
HAPPINESS	Body, mind, and soul harmonious responses
FEAR	Body and mind distorted responses
ANGER	Body and mind distorted responses
SHAME	Mind distorted responses
SURPRISE	Body and mind distorted responses
JOY	Soul, body and mind natural responses
AVERSION	Body and mind distorted responses
SADNESS	Body and mind distorted responses

Appendix III

TABLE OF PROGRAMMED BELIEFS

About me	About others	About the world
I do it wrong.	People must keep their promises.	People are destroying the planet.
I am bad.	People should not lie.	Something bad is going to happen.
I am a failure.	People should respect me.	Governments should do better.
I need to know.	They should listen to me.	There should not be wars.
I am right.	People are not grateful.	The world is not a safe place.
I need money.	Women are too emotional.	Life has a meaning.
I could make a mistake.	Men are too selfish.	People should be …
I am being rejected.	People should not suffer.	Business is business.
I have to work hard.	Members of families should love each other.	There is not enough for all.
I am too short, fat, ugly, slim, or tall.	I will make you happy.	Punishment and pain are sometimes necessary.
I have to control.	I know what others think.	Desire and ego are bad.
I have no power.	Others judge me.	Life is difficult.
It is my fault.	It was done wrong.	Animals should not suffer.
I know what to do.	People are useless, incompetent.	There is not enough time.

---

*   Some of the most commonly programmed beliefs

I need to understand.	People should not get angry.	Money is the problem.
I am not trust worthy.	I know what is good for you.	The world is not a safe place.
I could look stupid.	Others can hurt me.	The world will never change.
I am worthless.	I need you.	God is a fiction; otherwise, He would not allow suffering and pain.
I should be healthy.	I can change their minds.	Humans are not capable.
I need to decide.	You need me.	The world needs fixing.
I do not belong here.	I should not trust others.	We should all agree.
I attract negative things.	I know what should be done.	It is useless.
I don't know what to do.	Others should agree.	Life is not fair.
I have bad karma to pay.	I will disappoint people.	There is no time
I know what is best for me.	I am not important.	We are victims.
I need a relationship.	Others do not trust me.	Employers should be fair.
I missed my chance.	They should appreciate me	There is no solution.

Appendix IV

EXAMPLE OF HOW TO RESPOND TO THE INTERVIEW

Interview with Your Self

Section One

Situation: Politics and the financial situation are distressing. I worry about having trouble paying my bills.

Body (with regards to the situation you are concerned with consider the following:)

1) What part of my body am I more often aware of? Why do I think that is?
   Response: I feel oppression in my chest and a weight in my stomach. I think it's because I am so worried.

2) What part of my body might I be neglecting because of this? Why do I think that is?
   Response: I just noticed that my right shoulder also feels tense. I am stressed and tired most of the time.

3) What emotions are engaging me in an emotional reaction with regards to this?
Response: I am very afraid; I can't see a solution. It's been two years now and things are worse. It's not getting any better.

4) Where in my body do I feel a disconnection when thinking about this situation? Close your eyes and search for the sensations arising in your body.
Response: I'm disconnected with my feet and legs, the lower part of my body.

5) What physical activities am I experiencing issues with because of this situation? (Consider sleep, eating issues, pain issues, exercising, working, relaxing, and relating to others.)
Response: I'm not hungry and don't sleep well; I'm not keeping up with my exercise routines, and I have problems relaxing.

6) Who or what has been triggering my emotional responses as a result of this situation?
Response: Everyone is complaining, and the media always brings us bad news.

7) What do I spend most of my day doing with regards to the situation? (Reflect on money, time, energy, effort put forth, and sabotage.)
Response: I've been studying my finances, looking at ways to make things better, and looking at ways to increase sales.

8) What activities make me feel physically drained?
Response: Work is physically and mentally exhausting; I have no time for anything else. I don't feel up to doing anything when I get home.

9) How do I think my environmental surroundings are affecting this situation?
Response: The morale in my office has declined. Therefore, my environment isn't helping.

Situation: Politics and the financial situation are distressing. I worry about having trouble paying my bills.

Mind

1) What thoughts are occupying most of my mental space at the moment? (List a minimum of three and a maximum of six.)
Response: It's useless; I have no control, and something bad is going to happen.

2) Do I see any connection between the above thoughts?
Response: Yes, all are connected to my worries about the future.

3) Can I identify any of them playing a role in the situation? Could I choose one as most influential?
Response: Not feeling that I have any control in the situation.

4) What is my first thought in the morning and my last thought at night?
Response: Another day that I didn't sleep well; I'm going to be tired again with clients all day.

5) What thought is affecting my relationship with other(s)? (Scarcity, jealousy, envy, angry thoughts, sadness)
Response: Scarcity. I don't have enough money and am having trouble increasing sales.

6) How is this thought affecting my relationship with other(s)?
Response: I avoid going anywhere because I spend money when going out with friends. I don't see anyone, apart from clients and colleagues.

7) What are the excuses, logic, and planning running through my mental screen? Could any of them be creating the situation?
Response: I should look for another job, but when the weekend comes, I'm so exhausted that I don't feel up to it.

8) How does this situation match my story? (Past experiences, projected future, observing the world, others)
Response: Every time I get a job that pays well, something bad happens that I can't control; now the market is affected by the financial crisis.

The last time the company was in crisis, I spent a year looking for a job before I could leave. I spent every weekend filling in job applications.

It was the same when I opened my first business; it was bad timing in the midst of a recession, so I lost money and precious time.

9) What ideas are making me feel bad, weak, or overloaded? (Mental images)
Response: I don't see a solution; there's nothing I can do. If things don't improve, I could end up living with my parents again.

Situation: Politics and the financial situation is distressing. I worry about having trouble paying my bills.

Soul (When responding to the questions, you should try to get into the most honest response; go with your gut feeling.)

1) Do the ideas I hold about this situation come from any of the dualistic limitations, such as love/hate, good/bad, pleasure/pain, justice/injustice, and so on?
Response: It's not fair that this is happening, and it is very painful.

2) Are these ideas true and relevant to me, or could they be the influence of society, friends, and information you've studied through TV, religious beliefs, etc?
Response: Yes, they're relevant, because the events on the TV also affect me. I'm deeply affected by the crisis.

3) Are these ideas pushing me towards damaging actions, thoughts, and/or emotions for others and/or myself?

Response: Yes, sleepless nights, pain in my body, sadness, frustration, and anger towards the government and Wall Street.

4) When I panic or feel bad, how do I think this situation will turn out? (What does my intuition say v. my internal chatter?)
Response: I'll lose my home and be forced to move back to my parent's home in Kentucky.

5) Are my ideas, plans, and actions a quick fix, rather than a fearless, egoless response? Do these ideas, plans, and actions allow for spontaneity, synchronicity, or changes?
Response: I need to search for another job, and allow for a new or better job to come into my life.

6) How are these ideas affecting me now at an inner level? Do they feel right? Do they hold traces of old beliefs on karma, suffering, and learning struggles?
Response: I feel I have bad luck; I'm not sure about karma, but life always seems to be a struggle for me.

7) How do they separate me from the here and now? Do they enable me to get on with what is being placed in from of me? (Worrying about tomorrow, yesterday, and what if?)
Response: I'm thinking of the future all of the time.

8) How do I imagine myself responding or acting (or not) on this situation? If I were emotionally detached from its final outcome or result, how would that feel? Can I feel any resistance?
Response: I would be more relaxed and rested, and would feel more like going home and looking for jobs in sales, marketing, and even in teaching.

9) If I consider what I know deep within, what will then be my idea of this situation?
Response: This too shall pass; it will all turn out fine. It is just a matter of time.

Section Two

Situation: I now have a new job that pays better; I'm teaching, selling, and marketing, all of which I wanted to do.

Body

1) How does this situation feel in my body and levels of energy?
   Response: I'm energized and I am having fun at work. I feel excited.

2) What changes in physical activities have I made so that my body feels well?
   Response: I go to the gym every morning. I'm beginning to feel and look great.

3) When visualizing this outcome of the situation, what part of my body do I feel most connected to during the day?
   Response: My heart feels released of worry and my body has new energy.

4) In what physical activities would I most enjoy participating?
   Response: I love to go swimming and hiking with friends, like I used to.

5) Where in the world do I see myself living and spending most of my time?
   Response: I would live in Arizona, somewhere near the red rocks.

6) Who would make me feel relaxed and loved? It can be more than one person, or even a pet.
   Response: I would have a partner and two Labrador Retrievers.

7) How would I spend my time and activities related to work and leisure?
   Response: I would be teaching and selling on a part-time basis, and learning more about marketing in general.

8) How do I see myself spending my money—on what type of goods, energy, or quality of time?
Response: I'm renting a nice house; I eat healthy, organic foods, and enjoy life with my new partner.

9) Where in my body do I feel gratitude, peace, and joy?
Response: I'm happy and grateful, and I feel it in my heart

Situation: I now have a new job that pays better, and I'm teaching, selling, and marketing, all of which I wanted to do.

Mind

1) What thoughts occupy most of my mental space? List a minimum of three and a maximum of six.
Response: I'm inspired, I'm doing well, and I have a great future ahead of me.

2) What emotions would these thoughts trigger in me?
Response: Excitement more energy, and happiness.

3) What do I think would be my first thought and last thought every day?
Response: I would be happy to have my partner with me and grateful for my work.

4) How do I think these thoughts would affect my relationships?
Response: I would be good company, would make new friends, and would be kind and loving to all.

5) How is my logic (rationale) working best in order to create more of these experiences? (Trusting, service, love, compassion, giving, etc.)
Response: It would make me feel more patient, loving, and trusting.

6) How does this situation fit with my personal life experience (give three examples)?

Response: When I'm relaxed, I'm normally very loving and trusting with clients and colleagues, because I enjoy what I do.
I'm a good partner when I am not worried or stressed.
I'm involved in many social activities. When I'm worry-free, I'm fun and outgoing.

7) What ideas and images are the most empowering in this experience?
Response: The images of having new work, a new partner, and a completely new life experience.

8) How do I help others to experience similar situations?
Response: I can be more optimistic and outgoing by sharing them.

9) How do others help me in this situation?
Response: They give me their support; if I'm having down time, I know I can count on them to remind me of who I really am.

Situation: I now have a new job that pays better, and I'm teaching, selling, and marketing, all of which I wanted to do.

Soul

1) How will this situation make me feel in the long term, and will it still matter?
Response: I believe I'll feel better, but in the long run, it won't matter at all.

2) Now that things have turned around, what do I value most in this experience?
Response: I've learned that everything resolves itself in one way or another if we just go with the flow.

3) From where I stand now, what would I wish to do for others?
Response: To be more supportive and not so self-centered.

4) What would I like to do first, second, and third?
Response: Enjoy my new job, my partner, and my new location.

5) How will I express my unique gifts?
   Response: Teaching the skills I am good at, working hard, and learning more marketing techniques. I enjoy learning new things; I could also become certified as a hiking teacher.

6) Where in my daily activities and interactions can I express them?
   Response: At work and in my hobbies.

7) What will be my spiritual practice?
   Response: I'll do these interview questions and meditate at the rocks.

8) What would be my personal slogan or mantra? What defines how I see myself and my gifts?
   Response: Everything has a reason; relax and write about what you prefer. Then, once you know, act on it.

9) In what way do the above offer a fulfilling and engaging perspective of my life?
   Response: They've helped me to change my perspective; that's why everything has changed for the better.

I see that when I allow negative thinking, my body reacts by becoming sick. I feel tired and get less and less done. I must stop engaging in these thoughts and see them simply as clouds going by. I must not dwell on what I don't want, for that is exactly what I will get. Doing the interview has made clear for me what I prefer, along with other options. Now I can take action according to what I prefer, and not do something I should avoid.

Appendix V

EXAMPLE OF HOW TO RESPOND TO AN EXPRESS VERSION

Express Version of The Interview

A. Body (I'm fed-up with feeling overwhelmed with others and work; no one understands.)

1) I want to feel good and worry free v. nervous and exhausted.
2) I want to have all the money I need v. having to borrow from banks or others.
3) I want to do work I enjoy v. not having enough sales and clients.

B. Mind (I am fed-up with feeling overwhelmed with others and work; no one understands.)

1) I want to feel at ease and relaxed v. having everything and everyone upset me.
2) I want to feel peace and kindness in my life v. feeling impatient and moody.
3) I do stimulating things v. doing routine, automated tasks.

C. Soul (I'm fed up with feeling overwhelmed with others and work; no one understands.)

1) I want to have new friends and a new job v. accepting the status quo.
2) I want to trust myself fully all of the time v. feeling paralyzed and afraid.
3) I have clarity and am at peace v. being confused and doubtful.

Glossary

Acupuncture: A discipline that is part of Chinese medicine. It applies stimulation to different energetic points within the human in the body using different tools, either by inserting needles or staples to the skin.

Ady Shankara: Hindu philosopher from Kerala, India. His works helped the consolidation of Vedanta (see Vedanta). His work was written in the ancient Sanskrit language and based on the teachings of the *Upanishads*.

Annamaya: (See also koshas) One of the five sheaths (pancha-koshas) that makes reference to the body made of food that we refer to as the physical body.

Archetypical: A term that refers to a prototype, model or pattern from which other things with common characteristics derive. The word *archétypon* refers in Greek is the original mold. For psychoanalyst C. G. Jung, these archetypes or first prototypes were also in the collective unconscious, and he strongly believed they influenced an individual behavior and mind.

Advaita Vedanta: Considered the oldest school of Vedanta based on the *Upanishads*. The term can be translated into English as "nonduality."

Atman: The Sanskrit term used to refer to spirit, inner self, or soul.

Ayurveda: India's traditional system of medicine. The word Ayurveda could be translated into the "art of living." In Ayurveda, mind, body, and soul are interconnected and influence each other.

Buddhism: Based on the teachings of the Buddha (also known as Siddhartha Gautama). Buddhism has developed into different traditions and practices, some more religious and others more philosophical.

Chakras: Also known as part of the energetic body. This makes reference to the energy (Prana and Kundalini) centers of the body.

Charaka: The Ayurvedic, herbal pharmacopedia; it's the classical medical text and was written by Charak Samhita.

Chinese Medicine: As its name states, this body of medicine originated in China. Like Ayurveda, it also contains herbal recipes, massage techniques, exercises, dietary guides, and the practice of acupuncture.

Dharma: A term widely used in Hinduism and Buddhism. It makes reference to different things depending on the context; it could refer to a religion or a duty. This Sanskrit word conveys that which keeps things in an orderly, supportive manner in relation to the principles of life and the universe. According to Buddhism and Hinduism, each individual has a personal duty or path to follow.

DNA: Stands for the deoxyribonucleic acid that is in the genetic tissue of all living systems. It contains total information on a living organism, and is like a big memory file with biological instructions.

Doshas: Central part of Ayurvedic medicine, this Sanskrit word can be used for humor (state of mind andbody) that keep a person in balance. Ayurveda considers the body to be a dynamic system, not a solid thing. The dynamics are influenced by the three doshas: Vata, Pitta, and Kapha.

Gnostics: A thought system maintaining that the only path to the soul is the realization of Gnosis (esoteric or intuitive knowledge). It holds that the material world was created by a third party of demiurge, a negative being. It is similar to other religious systems that profess the belief in evil or Satan.

Hinduism: The predominant religion of the Indian subcontinent. It includes Shivaism, Vaishbavism, Smartism, and many other traditions. It contains laws and instructions for the practice of daily morals.

I Ching: Said to be the oldest Chinese classical text. Can be (and is mostly used) as an oracle. It's also been used to gain understanding and inner guidance about the evolution of relationships and change.

Illuminati: Translates as "enlightened;" this has been used to name groups both real and fictitious. The origins trace back to the Bavarian region (south Germany) where the Illuminati were founded in the seventeenth century. They opposed superstitions and religious ideas that influenced much of the contemporary public life, even to the point of abuse.

Kapha: One of the three doshas or humors from Ayurveda. It is the more solid and substantial of the three doshas, as it is made up of the elements of water and earth.

Karma: Sanskrit word that literally means action or doing. It also refers to the concept central to the law of moral cause and effect, and is fundamental in Buddhism and Hinduism.

Kinesiology: The study of human and animal motion and function. Kinesiology differs from applied kinesiology that the author refers to in this work. The second holds that every organ dysfunction is accompanied by a weakness in a specifically corresponding muscle.

Koshas: Sanskrit word that refers to the layers or five sheaths covering the Atman (soul) sheath. These have often been compared and referred to as the layers of an onion.

Layers of Life: It refers to the Kosha (see above) system, as in Ayurveda and Yoga philosophy. It refers to the nature of human beings that includes the physical and psychological aspects, as well as the collective and personal aspects. These can vary from the dense, physical aspects of the body to the more subtle layers of emotions, mind, and spirit.

Maya: Most often translated as the illusionary vision of the world created by our senses. Mainly, it is used to express the idea of a person's experience or perception that can be or is confused by the reality.

Mannomaya Kosha: It refers to layer that comes from the Sanskrit word, manas. It works with our five senses, and as such, it assists in forming our interpretation or perception of the world and its events. In Hindu and Buddhist traditions, this is also the greatest human obstacle to obtaining liberation (Moksha).

Mantras: Sanskrit term translating as "instrument of the mind;" it could be a sound, syllable, word, or group of words. The primordial mantra is Aum (Om), which is known as the creating or vibrational force. Mantras are considered spiritually powerful and transformational.

Moksha: It means release or liberation in many traditions, and is known as the liberation from rebirth or samsara,—the wheel of life. Samsara originated with new religious movements in the first millennium; the movements saw human life as a repeating process of birth and rebirth. One must achieve Moksha in order to be released from this cycle and its inherent suffering.

Neuropeptides: Peptides in the brain that influence its activity. They are involved in a wide range of brain functions: memory, learning, social behavior, reproduction pleasure/pain, metabolism, and food intake. Neuropeptides are related to peptide hormones (see peptides).

Nirvana: Sanskrit term that means "blown out;" it refers to a deep and stable peace of mind that is acquired through moksha (liberation). In Hinduism, it involves the union with Brahma (the supreme being).

Paradigm: Term used in the theory of knowledge and science to describe different labels, concepts, ideas, logic and thought patterns.

Peptides: Hormones secreted from neuroendocrine cells. These travel through the blood to distant tissues in the form of a response to some stimuli or bodily reaction. Neuropeptides are located in the brain; peptide hormones are not. However, the same enzymes synthesize both.

Pitta: One of the three Ayurvedic doshas or humors. It has transformation expression, such as from heat into water. The force expressing the transformative power of nature, it is made up mostly of the fire element and a part of the water element.

Prana: Vital force (see pranamaya kosha). The force that permeates the entire person and is the energy that holds the person together. Once this stops running through, the life ceases to be.

Pranamaya Kosha: (See layers of life) This term refers to the sheath or layer that is in the form of energy or vital force principle. It animates, vitalizes, and holds the body and the mind together. Its physical expression is the breath.

Psyche: Most commonly held term used to make reference to the self (conscious and unconscious) that is central to psychology and psychoanalysis. The root of the Greek word refers to the life force or breath and has derived meanings such spirit, soul, and self.

Reincarnation: The concept that a soul or a spirit will begin a new life after death in a new human or animal body. Depending on the moral quality of a person's life actions (Karma), the wheel of Samsara will go on in a determined path.

Rishis: Sanskrit term referring to a sage or wise man. A rishi is one who practices self-realization through yogic practice. His goal is to attain union with Brahma. The Rishi's soul knowledge and wisdom are received directly from the universal source.

Sannsyasin: A follower of a practice who has taken vows to live a celibate life, alone or in a community, but remains detached of possessions. The goal of the Sannsyasin is moksha liberation. Practices may involve meditation, yoga, or bhakti (devotional) meditation, according to the tradition; it will also include prayers.

Sanskrit: Language developed from Vedic Sanskrit primarily used as a ceremonial or liturgical language of Hinduism; it is also used by Buddhism scholars today.

Shankhya: One of the schools of Hindu philosophy, it is strongly dualistic and focuses on Moksha (liberation).

Shivaism: The most widely followed sect of Hinduism, which reveres the god Shiva as the supreme being.

Scientology: Religious movement created by science fiction writer, L. Ron Hubbard. It has been referred to by its opponents or critics as manipulative and deceptive. This is mainly due to its attempts to use science to expand human potential. Scientologists also believe that human beings on this planet originate from extraterrestrial beings.

Tao: (Dao) A Chinese concept for the way or path, Tao refers to the primordial essence or fundamental nature of the universe. Tao originated with Lao Tzu.

Taoism: A belief or thought system for which existence has no limits, no beginning, and no end. The concepts of death and birth are only part of a flow. Many original concepts of Tao are also shared in Zen, Confucianism, and Buddhism.

Upanishads: Consists of a collection of philosophical texts, which form the theoretical basis for the Hindu religion, also known as Vedanta (see Vedanta).

Vata: One of the three Ayurvedic doshas or humors that refers to the movement in the human body and mind. It is made up of the space and wind elements and, as such, it has a more subtle nature.

Vedanta: (See also Advaita.) It is the part of the Veda that deals with knowledge and truth. In the post-medieval period in India, Vedanta was the dominant school of thought.

Vortex: In energy, it describes a powerful force drawing into its current everything that surrounds it, like in a black hole.

Ying/Yang: Duality, as expressed in the Chinese concept of opposites. The difference is that the Chinese concept of ying/yang also implies that, although opposite or contrary, these forces are interdependent in the natural world. Ying expresses and represents female attributes and characteristics, while yang expresses its opposite, the masculine.

Zen: A philosophy that has its origins in China, but flourished in Japan. It is a branch of Buddhism that is also involved in the attainment of enlightenment referred to as Satori. Its method involves following a strict and close guidance of a Zen Master who uses paradox to challenge the Zen student.

Bibliography

Anthony, K. Carol and Moog, Hanna. *I Ching: The Oracle of the Cosmic Way*, ICHINGBOOKS; First edition (Aug. 16 2011) Sold by: Amazon Digital Services, Inc. e-book edition 2011.

Chamberlain, David. *The Mind of Your Newborn Baby.* Berkeley: North Atlantic Books, 1998.

Chopra, Deepak MD. *Perfect Health, The Complete Mind/Body Guide.* Published by Three Rivers Press New York, New York, Revised Edition 2000. Originally Published in hardcover by Harmony Books 199, printed in the USA.

Braden, Greg. *Secrets of the Lost Mode of Prayer, The Hidden Power of Beauty, Blessings, Wisdom Hurt.* Hay House, Carlsbad California, USA, January 2006.

Byron, Katie. *Loving What Is: Four Questions that Can Change Your Life.* New York: Three Rivers Press, 2002.

Dyer, Wayne. W. *La Fuerza del Espiritu.* Traduccion Carme Camps (Spanish Edition) by Grijalbo Mondadory, Barcelona, Spain 2001.

Faust, Michael. *Eastern Religion for Western Gnostics.* Hyperreality Books, Miami, Florida, USA 2010.

Gaynor, Mitchell L. *Sonidos Que Curan: Descubra el poder terapéutico del Sonido, la Voz y La Música* (en papel), Editorial URANO, 2001.

Tolle, Eckhart. *A New Earth*. New York: Namaste Publishing, 2005.

Osho, The Osho Transformation; *Tarot, Insights and Parables for Renewal in Everyday Life*. St. Martin's Press, New York, New York, USA, December 1999.

Pert, Candace (PhD). *The Biology of Emotions, Why You Feel the Way You Feel*. Touchstone New York, 1999.

Ram Dass and Rameshwar, Das. *Be Love Now, The Path of the Heart*. London: Rider, 2010.

Ram Dass and Goleman, Daniel. *Journey of Awakening, A Meditator's Guidebook*. New York: Bantam Books, 1990.

Walsch, Neale D. *Bringers of the Light. How You can Change Your Life and Change the World*. Milenium Legacies Inc. Ashland, OR, 1995.

Walsch, Neale D. *Conversations with God: An Uncommon Dialogue (Book 1)* Penguin Group (USA) Incorporated NY 1996.

Walsch, Neale D. *When Everything Changes, Change Everything. In time of Turnoil a Pathway to Peace*. Hampton Roads Publishing, Charlottesville VA, 2009.

Walter, "Sanntree" Kacera, D.N., PhD. *Ayurvedic Tongue Diagnosis*. Motilal Delhi: Banarsidass Publishers Private Limited, 2006.

Yogananda, Paramhansa. *Spiritual Relationships*. Cristal Clarity Publishers, Nevada City, CA, 2007.

Made in the USA
Middletown, DE
05 July 2016